THE BOOKS
THAT MATTERED

THE BOOKS
THAT MATTERED

A Reader's Memoir

FRYE GAILLARD

NEWSOUTH BOOKS
MONTGOMERY

NewSouth Books
105 S. Court Street
Montgomery, AL 36104

Library of Congress Cataloging-in-Publication Data

Gaillard, Frye, 1946–
The books that mattered : a reader's memoir / Frye Gaillard.

pages cm

ISBN-13: 978-1-58838-287-0 (alk. paper)
ISBN-10: 1-58838-287-7 (alk. paper)

1. Gaillard, Frye, 1946—-Books and reading. 2. Books and reading—
United States. 3. Books and reading—Psychological aspects. I. Title.
Z1003.2.G35 2012
028'.90973—dc23

2012012229

Design by Victoria Hartman

This book was typeset in Adobe Janson Text, with
embellishments in Zapf Dingbats and Adobe Wood Type.

Printed in the United States of America by
Edwards Brothers Malloy

To Julie Suk,
the poet in the family

✦

And to Nancy

"The poet's voice need not merely be the record of man, it can be one of the props, the pillars to help him endure and prevail."

— WILLIAM FAULKNER

"Stories are the only enchantment possible, for when we begin to see our suffering as a story, we are saved. It is the balm of the primitive, the way to exorcise a terrifying life."

— ANAIS NIN

"I think you must remember that a writer is a simple-minded person to begin with . . . He's not a great mind, he's not a great thinker, he's not a great philosopher, he's a storyteller."

— ERSKINE CALDWELL

Contents

Prologue

L AST YEAR I was re-reading some favorite books, including Charles Dickens's *A Tale of Two Cities*, always, for me, one of the most durable of the classics. *It was the best of times, it was the worst of times* . . . Such a fine setup for a novel of upheaval and social injustice, a warning by Dickens against the flaws in European society. Somehow, maybe because I once read them in consecutive weeks, it is a book associated in my mind with Walker Percy's *Love in the Ruins*, in which the protagonist, Dr. Thomas More, a psychiatrist and mental patient in the same institution, is contemplating the possibility of anarchy.

Now in these dread latter days of the old violent beloved U.S.A. and of the Christ-forgetting Christ-haunted death-dealing Western world I came to myself in a grove of young pines and the question came to me: has it happened at last?

Two more hours should tell the story. One way or the other. Either I am right and a catastrophe will occur, or it won't and I'm crazy. In either case the outlook is not so good.

Once again, not a bad beginning for a book.

I was subsequently talking about these things—favorite books and why they move us—with my friend, Jay Lamar, director of the Caroline Marshall Draughon Center for the Arts and Humanities at Auburn University. Jay is, and has been for years, one of the most important figures in the Alabama literary scene, a writer and editor who also plays a catalytic role. For some years now, through her programming at the center, she has brought writers and readers together in college classrooms, community centers, libraries, and other venues to talk about the things that matter to us all.

In one of my conversations with Jay, I mentioned that I had always wanted to write a book about books, those that had brought me the greatest delight through the years. I wanted to offer a reader's tribute, but more than that, a kind of reader's *memoir*, a recounting of exactly why and when these volumes had mattered. I think I may have mentioned *The Plague* by Albert Camus, a book that I found to be curiously inspiring, given the dismal subject matter. For the narrator and central character, Dr. Bernard Rieux, there is meaning on the other side of suffering, and when I read the book as a college freshman I remember clinging to that glimmer of hope.

I'm sure that I also mentioned William Faulkner, not a writer that I always enjoyed, but one who provided the very definition of art—the human heart in conflict with itself—and a reason to consider why reading mattered. Jay encouraged me to go ahead with the book, while she and other members of her staff developed programming to go along with it. In the pages that follow are eleven essays featuring thirty-odd books, both fiction and non, that have had a major impact on my life. This list (it was supposed to be a Top 25, but it grew) is not my estimate of the thirty best books ever written, but simply those that have mattered most to me.

Some conspicuous names are missing. There is no Shakespeare, no Dostoevsky, no Hemingway or Thomas Mann, or for that matter, no Barbara Kingsolver. It is also true that some of these selections are personal indeed. I doubt if most such lists would include Larry L. King's *The Old Man and Lesser Mortals*, or Jacobo Timerman's *The Longest War*, or Lillian Smith's *Killers of the Dream*, as beautifully written as these books are. And most fans of David Halberstam would be more likely to choose *The Best and the Brightest* over *The Unfinished Odyssey of Robert Kennedy*. But there are some books that I suspect would make a lot of lists: *To Kill a Mockingbird*, *Adventures of Huckleberry Finn*, perhaps *The Grapes of Wrath* or *All the King's Men*—none of these are especially original selections, but they come from the heart.

My hope is that those who read this book, or participate in the programming that is scheduled to follow (either regional or national, under the auspices of the Caroline Marshall Draughon Center for the Arts and Humanities) will be moved not to adopt these selections but rather to create an equally personal list. I have to say that in more than forty years as a writer, I've never been involved in a more satisfying project, or one more fun, and I'm happy now to let it go forth, hoping, expecting, that those of you who thumb through the pages will be moved to contagious ruminations of your own.

THE BOOKS
THAT MATTERED

· 1 ·

Once Upon a Time

FEATURING:

Johnny Tremain—Esther Forbes

Adventures of Huckleberry Finn—Mark Twain

ALSO, TONI MORRISON, RALPH ELLISON,
ROY BLOUNT JR., RON POWERS

I

MY FIRST ENCOUNTERS with books were disappointing.

I remember when I was a very little boy thumbing through the pages of fairy tales, which were, as far as I could tell, stories of cannibalism and mayhem in which giants and witches, tigers and wolves did their best to eat small children. Then came school and the announcement that I must learn to read, and the books they gave us to accomplish this task were as dull and dreary as the fairy tales had been terrifying. *This is Spot. See Spot run.* I wondered what these people were thinking. Whatever happened to the idea of a *story*? This was something I knew all about, for I had a favorite aunt—her name was Mary, but

3

I called her Mamie—who had a gift for telling fine tales, which had the advantage that they were mostly true.

Mamie lived in the house next door to ours, and it seemed to be filled with the whisper of old ghosts. Not the scary kind, but the benevolent presence of a rich family past that wound its way back into hazy and unfamiliar places that we could only see in our minds. The house itself was a source of endless fascination for me, and for my cousin, who came to visit most often in the summer. We loved the nooks and crannies of the attic, where we sometimes sifted through the moth-eaten relics, old coats and dresses that my cousin loved, and a Confederate jacket that had once been worn by a member of the family.

Everything about the place was antebellum, but not in the Gone-With-the-Wind, Greek revival tradition with the great white columns and curving staircases; this was, instead, an unpretentious two-story house built to catch the summer breeze—a Gulf Coast cottage, constructed by slaves in 1836. It was surrounded by magnolias and oak trees draped with Spanish moss and azaleas blooming pink at the first hint of spring. Mamie roamed those grounds with great satisfaction, and welcomed an extended family of children into this curious world of memory. I remember sitting with her on the front porch swing when I was maybe five or six, my cousin Julie on one side, me on the other, while she told us stories of the Revolutionary War.

Her favorite subject was General Francis Marion, "the Swamp Fox" as he was then known, a Low Country-patriot from South Carolina with whom Peter Gaillard, one of our own ancestors, had ridden. "A plague on that wily Swamp Fox!" she would cry, imitating Cornwallis or some other British general driven to distraction by Marion's bold guerilla raids. For me as a child, listening to her stories was pure joy, and at least for the first ten years of my life it simply never occurred to me that anything this good could happen in a book.

But then I discovered *Johnny Tremain*. I must have been in the fourth grade, and there it was on a library shelf, imposing in its mass at more than two hundred pages. Later, I would learn about its author, how Esther Forbes, a remarkably prolific writer from Boston, had won acclaim for her novels and a Pulitzer Prize in the 1940s for a biography she had written of Paul Revere. For *Johnny Tremain*, a story for young readers about the Revolutionary War, she had won the Newbery Medal in 1944, and even now her book is remembered as one of the finest children's novels ever written.

For me, it was magic. It was the tale of a boy in Revolutionary Boston, a silversmith's apprentice initially unaware, at the age of fourteen, of the turbulent history taking shape around him. He lived in the attic of his master's house, sharing cramped quarters with two other boys, both far less gifted than he. I think I was drawn to this flawed hero, Johnny Tremain, precisely because the author had not made him perfect. He seemed so real in his flashes of arrogance and disdain, so completely believable to a reader like me, just a few years younger and thus drawn easily into his world. And what a world it was!

There was only one window in the attic. Johnny always stood before it as he dressed. He liked this view down the length of Hancock's Wharf. Counting houses, shops, stores, sail lofts, and one great ship after another, home again after their voyaging, content as cows waiting to be milked. He watched the gulls, so fierce and beautiful, fighting and screaming among the ships. Beyond the wharf was the sea and the rocky islands where the gulls nested.

As Esther Forbes's story unfolds, so does a vivid portrait of a time in which the people of Boston are much like the gulls—scrapping to feed their families and themselves. Yet they also know there are opportunities in America that the Mother Country could never offer.

For their working-class counterparts across the Atlantic, there was far less hope of anything better, far less chance of upward mobility, no matter their ambition or grit.

In Boston, seething with life and a ferocious sense of greater possibility, a resourceful boy like Johnny Tremain could indenture his services to a master craftsman, knowing that one day he would have his own shop. For a time that was all Johnny thought about, encouraged in his dreams by the great Paul Revere, one of the finest silversmiths in the city. But then without warning, his expectations ended in calamity. As Johnny was rushing one morning to fill an order, a crucible containing molten silver cracked from the strain of too much heat, and the liquid metal quickly coated his hand, burning his delicate flesh so severely that his thumb became welded to the edge of his palm. Even after he recovered from the pain, and the fever and delirium that went along with it, he knew that his days as a silversmith were over. For a time he wandered the piers of Boston, trying to imagine another way of life but finding nothing to compare with what had abruptly been taken from him.

He rarely bothered to look at the signs over the door which indicated what work was done inside. A pair of scissors for a tailor, a gold lamb for a wool weaver, a basin for a barber, a painted wooden book for a bookbinder, a large swinging compass for an instrument-maker . . . A butcher (his sign was a gilded ox skull) would have employed him, but the idea of slaughtering animals sickened him. He was a fine craftsman to the tips of his fingers—even to the tips of his maimed hand.

Finally, Johnny came upon a newspaper office, where he was offered a job delivering papers. He might have considered such work beneath him, except for the fact that it came with a horse—a spirited gelding with pale blue eyes, his coat nearly white but flecked with brown, and a mane and tale that were almost black. Johnny was impressed by the animal's beauty, and even more by his speed; but also by a timid, vulnerable spirit that required a gentle hand from the rider. Within a few days, horse and boy had developed a bond as they galloped through the rolling hills of Massachusetts, handing out papers from Boston all the way to Lexington and Concord.

The year was 1773, and Boston was the epicenter of rebellion—a fact that Johnny understood well. British troops now occupied the city, and flashes of violence seemed to happen every day. As he began to read the papers he delivered, studying the incendiary editorials, he developed a passion for the Patriot cause. He soon discovered that the attic just above the newspaper office was a place where the rebel leaders—John Hancock and Samuel Adams, Paul Revere and Joseph Warren—came and mapped their strategies of insurrection.

And so it was that Esther Forbes began to weave her tale of adventure through a history that had won her a Pulitzer Prize. The complexity of her achievement was beyond the understanding of a reader barely ten. Even so, I knew there was something in the way she told the story that went far beyond what I learned in school. Paul Revere, previously nothing more than a stick-figure legend, suddenly came alive in her pages—the robust son of an immigrant father, stocky in his build, swarthy in his look, a man who anchored a network of spies.

John Hancock, known to me only for his signature, emerged as a complicated character—one of the richest men in Massachusetts, with all of the vanity such wealth might imply, but a leader who was willing to risk everything for a cause in which he deeply believed. Along with Samuel Adams, an ally who could scarcely have been more different, Hancock was generally regarded by the British occupiers as one of the most dangerous men in the colonies. Adams, meanwhile, appeared in the pages of *Johnny Tremain* as a man who was never very good at anything, except politics.

Unlike John Adams, his more famous cousin, Sam was a patient, disheveled man in his early forties, prematurely gray, and content, it seemed, to let other men take center stage. His hands and voice often shook when he spoke, even as he planned the Boston Tea Party, but there was never any doubt—certainly not in the minds of the British—that his organizing genius lay at the heart of the Patriot cause.

But perhaps the most intriguing figure of all, and to me the least known, was Dr. Joseph Warren, a thirty-something physician who had achieved renown in the medical world through his belief in inoculations for small pox. The disease had ravaged Boston more than once, and in the great epidemic of 1764, Warren was able to demonstrate the value of his largely untested and controversial practice. One of those he inoculated was John Adams. As Boston drifted toward revolution, this gentle physician—"a fine-looking man," in the words of Esther Forbes, "with fresh skin and thick blond hair and very bright eyes"—emerged as a leader both fiery and fearless.

It was Warren who, on April 18, 1775, sent Paul Revere on his ride to Lexington and Concord—first to warn Sam Adams and John Hancock, who were then in Lexington, that the British army was on its way to arrest them. The other mission of the British that night was to seize the Patriot munitions in Concord, and it was there that the minutemen gathered in force.

Faced with a withering fire as they marched toward the village, the British regulars broke and ran—a possibility that had scarcely occurred to them, given the ragtag army they were facing. It was, of course, one of those inspiring moments of history that mutates easily into mythology, and I remember as a boy being stirred. But there was something in the quality of Esther Forbes's telling that suggested that this was a more subtle story, tinged, perhaps, with irony and pathos. Not that I formed such thoughts at the time. I was far too inspired by a newfound passion for history and books.

Many years later as I studied the Revolutionary War, I was prepared, I think, for the curious ambiguities of our founding—how the war slogged on for eight bloody years, and how George Washington's greatest gift was not his grasp of military strategy, but rather his ability, against all odds, simply to hold his army together. His soldiers' suffering at Valley Forge and other places was made even worse by the stinginess of American farmers, who sometimes charged outrageous prices for the food a desperate army had to have. And even the Founding Fathers themselves were capable of individual pettiness and possessed their collective feet of clay. Among other things, most of them understood the contradiction between their professions of liberty and the existence of chattel slavery.

"I can not, I will not, justify it," admitted Patrick Henry of Virginia. But neither he nor any of the others did much about it.

And yet I think I also knew as I came to the end of *Johnny Tremain* that I had read a carefully crafted account—an account that now had a heart and a face—of the founding of the greatest country in the world.

II

Whatever the subject, my parents were delighted by my new love of books, and since we were the last in the neighborhood to actually purchase our own TV, we began a tradition that lasted several years. The three of us—my mother, my father, and me, the only child— would gather together in our den at night and read to each other aloud, passing around the designated book, until finally one or more of us would get sleepy.

I think we may have begun with *Old Yeller*, or perhaps a novel by Zane Grey. But one of the readings I remember most clearly was *Eneas Africanus*, a vintage story from 1919 written by a Georgian, Harry Stillwell Edwards. It was a happy tale of slavery in which Eneas, an elderly slave, becomes separated from his master, and even after emancipation, searches eight years to find him. The book, which sold through forty Grosset & Dunlap editions, ends on a note of tender reunion:

In the red light of the bonfire an old negro suddenly appeared, reining up a splendid grey horse . . . His "Whoa, Chainlightnin!" resounded all over the place. Then he stood up and began to shout about Moses and the Hebrew children being led out of Egypt into the promised land. Major Tommey listened for a brief instant and rushed out. The newcomer met him with an equal rush and their loud greetings floated back to us clear as the notes of a plantation bell: "Eneas, you black rascal, where have you been?"

However startling the political incorrectness, we were a family in the 1950s who very much wanted to shore up the notion that nothing in particular was wrong with the South. The civil rights movement was beginning to stir just up the road from us in Montgomery, and Southern defensiveness—that massive, collective chip on the shoulder that had been around at least since the Civil War—took a lot of different forms. One of them, certainly, was a book on racial harmony and contentment, rooted in the gospel of white supremacy. As a boy of ten, I was deeply moved.

But then we came to Huckleberry Finn. It was another splendid story of adventure—another boy about the age of Johnny Tremain, caught in his own encounter with history. It was set, of course, in a wholly different time, as the America created so painfully by the founders drifted inexorably toward the Civil War. The driving force in the conflict was slavery, and in *Adventures of Huckleberry Finn* we confronted the issue through the rough-hewn innocence of a runaway boy. But not right away. As literary scholars have told us through the years, when Mark Twain began work on his masterpiece, he set out modestly to write a sequel to *The Adventures of Tom Sawyer*, a best seller published in 1876.

In the early drafts of *Huckleberry Finn*, Jim, the slave, who provides the novel with its moral and literary strength, is only a minor character. And even in the final version, published in 1884 after Twain had worked on it for nearly ten years, the ethical tension takes shape slowly. In the opening pages, the book is driven by loneliness and fear, a ragamuffin boy on the margins of society, terrified of abuse at the hands of his father, and scorned by the people in his small river town for his superstitious understanding of the world. Even as a boy myself, skipping along on the surface of the story, I was touched by the beauty of Huck's ruminations and the intimations of wisdom they contained.

I felt so lonesome I most wished I was dead. The stars was shining, and the leaves rustled in the woods ever so mournful; and I heard an owl, away off, who-whooing about somebody that was dead, and a whippowill and a dog crying about somebody that was going to die; and the wind was trying to whisper something to me and I couldn't make out what it was, and so it made the cold shivers run over me. Then away out in the woods I heard that kind of sound that a ghost makes when it wants to tell something that's on its mind and can't make itself understood, and so can't rest easy in its grave and has to go about that way every night grieving. I got so down-hearted and scared, I did wish I had some company.

Even now, I remember reading that passage aloud, or maybe it was my mother or father who read it. Whatever, I was swept up gently into Huck's place and time, able to hear what he heard, feel what he felt, and despite the sadness at the heart of the scene, there was also a serenity that came from the simple beauty of his words.

But it was soon disrupted by the character of Pap. Huck Finn's drunken, violent father was, for me, an archetype of pure malice who resurrected old terrors from the world of fairy tales. Pap, however, was not a giant or a witch. There was nothing unbelievable about him when he appeared one evening in Huck's room and threatened grave harm. Infuriated by people in the town who thought that Huck should have a better home, Pap took him to a cabin deep in the woods.

"It was pretty good times up in the woods there, take it all around," Huck recounted. "But by-and-by pap got too handy with his hick'ry, and I couldn't stand it. I was all over welts."

Then one night in a drunken rage Pap tried to kill him.

He chased me round and round the place, with a clasp-knife, calling me the Angel of Death and saying he would kill me and then I couldn't come for him no more. I begged, and told him I was only Huck, but he laughed such a screechy laugh, and roared and cussed, and kept on chasing me up. Once when I turned short and dodged under his arm he made a grab and got me by the jacket between my shoulders, and I thought I was gone; but I slid out of the jacket quick as lightning, and saved myself. Pretty soon he was all tired out, and dropped down with his back against the door, and said he would rest a minute and then kill me.

On my first encounter with the story, I read those words with a rush of pure fright, and the nerve-rattling tension only grew worse as Huck began to plan his escape. Locked in the cabin while his father went to town for supplies, he began to saw a hole through the logs, but would he make it in time? And after he made his dash to the river, would somebody see him in the canoe? For the next two hundred pages or more, one close scrape followed another, and I remember taking comfort in only one thing. I was glad that Huck had a little bit of company.

It began with an echo of *Robinson Crusoe*, Huck setting up camp on Jackson Island—a wooded, uninhabited patch of land just downriver from Hannibal, Missouri—then discovering suddenly that he was not alone. On a morning exploration he found a campfire, smoldering, only recently abandoned, and when he came back later, fearful and creeping through the dark, he saw that it was Jim, a runaway slave. "I bet I was glad to see him," said Huck, for Jim had been the property of Miss Watson, a woman in Hannibal who had previously taken it upon herself to see that Huck became "civilized." Jim and Huck had known each other and been friendly enough, and now for different reasons they were running away.

Jim, for his part, had overheard talk that he was about to be "sold down the river," sent away to somewhere down in Louisiana, and his desperate flight to avoid that fate had awakened feelings even more elemental. He felt a powerful need to be free.

As the two traveled together on a raft, dodging bounty hunters and outlaws, they began to develop the kind of friendship that was, in the words of Toni Morrison, "so free of lies it produces an aura of restfulness and peace unavailable anywhere else in the novel." I think it may have been that very thing that caught my fancy on the first of many readings—that and the palpable feeling of freedom as they floated the currents of the great Mississippi.

Sometimes we'd have that whole river all to ourselves for the longest time. Yonder was the banks and the islands, across the water; and maybe a spark—which was a candle in a cabin window—and sometimes on the water you could see a spark or two—on a raft or a scow, you know; and maybe you could hear a fiddle or a song coming over from one of them crafts. It's lovely to live on a raft.

And yet, again and again on the journey, despite the companionship of those moments, Huck is caught in his own private struggle—a conflict, as Mark Twain later put it, between "a sound heart and a deformed conscience." He knew he was helping a runaway slave, a sin and a crime by the standard of the times, and in a masterstroke of cultural satire, Twain has him agonize about that, accepting slavery, at least in his mind, as part of the natural order of things. Huck worries about what he's doing to Miss Watson, Jim's former owner, and worries that God, being white Himself, will send him to hell. "I about made up my mind to pray . . ." he says. "But the words wouldn't come . . . You can't pray a lie—I found that out."

Huck, in the end, is too caught up in his friendship with Jim, in the kindness and humanity that's he's learned to appreciate on the river, and thus he bows to his inevitable fate. "All right, then," he finally decides, "I'll *go* to hell . . ."

It is, of course, one of the iconic scenes in American literature, that kernel of greatness in *Huckleberry Finn* that has made it a classic of American letters. "It's the best book we've had," Ernest Hemingway once declared. "All American writing comes from that." And yet the story has always been double-edged. Ralph Ellison, one of the great black writers of the twentieth century, said that when he first read the novel as a boy, he could identify easily enough with Huck, but not with Jim, despite their common racial heritage. Jim, in his uncomplicated innocence, was a little too close to Harriet Beecher Stowe's Uncle Tom, or even worse, to Eneas Africanus, and thus it seemed to Ellison and others that Twain fell short on a fundamental task—"filling out the complex humanity" of a character who was indispensable to the story.

Robert O'Meally of Columbia University pushed a similar point even further. In an introduction to a 2003 edition of *Huckleberry Finn*, O'Meally recalled that as an African American student in the civil rights era, he first read the novel with great admiration. "Here was democracy without puffery," he wrote, "*e pluribus unum* at its most radical level of two friends from different racial (but very similar cultural) backgrounds loving one another . . ."

But even in the rush of that first reading, O'Meally was troubled by the figure of Jim. It was easy enough, he thought, to admire Jim's humanity, wisdom, and courage. But he urged readers to "resist the idea that Jim is thoroughly realistic, that black men of his time were typically this simplistic, docile, or full of minstrel-show-like patter." In the end he wondered with Ralph Ellison if Twain had simply discounted black readers, if *Huckleberry Finn* at the time it was published—and perhaps even now—was primarily a dialogue among whites.

In my own re-reading of this most studied of American novels (I read it for a second time in college, and have read it four or five times since), I find that I'm conscious on every occasion of the debates that surround it. Sometimes I think they get in the way, detract from the beauty and the heart of a story that's set inevitably in time. But I also came to believe through the years that these same debates underscored the power and the truth of the novel. At the very least, they made me want to know more about the author. And on that front a handful of modern scholars have excelled.

III

Time magazine, in a retrospective published in 2008, called "Mark Twain: Our Original Superstar." In addition to his renown as a writer,

Twain traveled the country in the latter half of the nineteenth century, delivering lectures to sold-out audiences. He could make them laugh simply by walking onto the stage, looking disheveled with his mop of curly hair, and delivering his own sarcastic commentary on the multiple hypocrisies of his time.

"We know his voice only from written descriptions of it," wrote humorist Roy Blount Jr. "It was resonant enough to hold a large lecture hall audience rapt. He spoke in a slow backwoods drawl, with many strategic pauses . . . But he wasn't the sort of funny man who laughs at his own jokes. In performance and in life, Twain's facial expression—except, presumably when he was furious, which was often—was deadpan. After Twain's death, the editor of the *North American Review* recalled that he had known him for thirty years and never seen him laugh."

The definitive chronicle of Twain's emergence as "the nation's first rock star" is probably Ron Powers's *Mark Twain: A Life*, a riveting, literary account, published in 2005. In the prologue of this fine work, Powers introduces his subject this way:

Mark Twain's great achievement as the man who found a voice for his country has made him a challenge for his biographers. His words are quoted, yet he somehow lies hidden in plain sight—a giant on the historic landscape. He has been so thoroughly rearranged and reconstructed by a long succession of scholarly critics that the contours of an actual, textured human character have been obscured.

In his attempt to remedy this lack of understanding, Powers begins, as many biographers might, with Twain's boyhood—with the days in antebellum Missouri when this most seminal of American authors was little Sammy Clemens, spending his early childhood years, not on the great Mississippi River but rather on a broad expanse of prairie. There, his hard-luck father, Marshall Clemens, who seemed to fail at everything he tried, owned a small farm with a handful of slaves. It was here, says Powers, that the future Mark Twain first developed those qualities that set him apart, his remarkable abilities to listen and to see.

The prairie in its loneliness and peace: that was what came back to him toward the end of his life . . . He thought not of the Mississippi River, which he encountered most fully later in life, but of "a level great prairie which was covered with wild strawberry plants, vividly starred with prairie pinks, and walled in on all sides by forests"—a swatch of great western carpet yet a decade from disfigurement by the grooves of the California gold rushers. There his prodigious noticing had begun. His way of seeing and hearing things that changed America's way of seeing and hearing things.

With a gift that ultimately could not be explained, Twain transformed "commonplace language" into art, feeling its rhythms, its colorful riffs and improvisations, much as a great musician playing jazz. And nowhere did he find those rhythms more lovely than among the slaves he knew as a child.

One in particular captured his fancy. Uncle Dan'l was a dark-skinned man of middle age, the father of most of the Negro children on the farm, and in the words of Twain himself, a person "whose sympathies were wide and warm, and whose heart was honest and simple and knew no guile." He was also a great storyteller, spinning his yarns for Sammy and his cousins, as well as the slave children gathered at his cabin. Uncle Dan'l's speaking prowess, particularly his strategic use of the pause, later influenced Twain's own style. More importantly, as Powers and other biographers have noted, this slave was also the model for Jim, and one of many in Sam's early years who left their mark on his racial understanding.

"I have no race prejudices," Twain later declared. "All I care to know is that a man is a human being—that is enough for me." And he added with an irony that became his trademark, "He can't be any worse."

It always seemed to me as a reader that the fundamental truth of Twain's self-assessment is reflected in the pages of *Huckleberry Finn*. But the issue, inevitably, is more complicated. As Powers, among others, is compelled to remind us, there was another experience in Twain's early years, another more disturbing influence he absorbed. When he was ten a minstrel show came to town, featuring an actor named Thomas "Daddy" Rice, who performed in blackface and created a character he called "Jim Crow"—a slave whose colorful buffoonery usually drew gales of laughter from the crowd. One of those who laughed was the future Mark Twain. As Ron Powers notes, Twain never got over the delight he took in the choreographed foolishness of "the real nigger show," and without any question in *Huckleberry Finn*, the character of Jim bears the taint of that memory. And there is also this: in the course of the novel, Twain used the n-word 219 times, thinking no more of it than did the masses of his readers in those closing years of the nineteenth century.

Thus, the modern debate over *Huckleberry Finn* has taken two forms. One is epitomized by the thoughtful ruminations of Toni Morrison, African American winner of the Nobel Prize, who is troubled by the flaws in the character of Jim, that interplay of heroism and unreality that came from the imagination of Mark Twain. She sees the limitations of Twain's understanding; he was, after all, a man who lived in another century, when the nation first struggled with the aftermath of slavery, and the notion of racial equality was new. But Morrison is also moved by the book, moved by the strength and goodness of Jim, the moral decency of Huck, and the searing satire that Twain offers up against the casual hypocrisies of his time.

But there is a second kind of argument over *Huckleberry Finn*, one that first appeared in the civil rights years, and continues to raise its head even now. It can be reduced essentially to political correctness. In this debate, we focus on the n-word, as we so often do in our racial discussions at large—as if by stamping it out, we could free ourselves from racism itself.

Unfortunately enough, the discomfort we feel with *Huckleberry Finn*—which has lasted now for more than a century—goes deeper than that; as a society we are still engaged, in one way or another, with the fundamental conflict of Huck himself. During his time of moral agony on the raft, when he knows he is helping Jim to escape, Huck's head and heart are locked in a struggle. His head, of course, blithely accepts the assumptions of his time: the rectitude of slavery and the racial inferiority of his friend. But his heart understands a much deeper truth: the humanity of Jim, and thus the lie at the heart of racism. Today, I think, it may well be that we have managed to reverse it. Our heads after so many years of struggle have almost gotten it straight, and thus Huck's dialogue with himself seems both disconcerting and foolish.

I tried to make out to myself that I warn't to blame, because I didn't run Jim off from his rightful owner; but it warn't no use, conscience up and says, every time, "But you knowed he was running for his freedom, and you could a paddled ashore and told somebody." That was so—I couldn't get around that noway.

Now here we are, re-reading all this in the twenty-first century—a time when an ugly xenophobia is sweeping through our national debate, and when leaders in the opposition party are demonizing our first black president—and *Huckleberry Finn*, so perpetually provocative, is still as unsettling to us as ever. If our heads have finally learned what's what, if, for example, most of us know not to use the n-word, I think that today it may be our hearts—our collective heart and soul as a nation—that we're still a little unsure of.

IV

It's true, of course, when I first read the book that I gave little thought to these kinds of issues. The great delight in *Huckleberry Finn*, just as it was with *Johnny Tremain*, was of seeing a story come alive on the pages. There seemed to be such magic in the telling, such joy in the dangers, such admiration for the pluck of both characters, and I knew right away that I had to have more.

Because of these gifts from Mark Twain and Esther Forbes, I understood clearly by the age of ten that books would be my companions for life—sometimes the *same* book, read again and again through the years. That most emphatically would be the case with my next great literary encounter—another multilayered tale of discovery, this one set even closer to home.

· 2 ·

Southern Voices

FEATURING:

To Kill a Mockingbird—Harper Lee

The Heart Is a Lonely Hunter—Carson McCullers

A Curtain of Green—Eudora Welty

Killers of the Dream—Lillian Smith

ALSO, JAMES AGEE, CHARLES J. SHIELDS,
FLANNERY O'CONNOR

I

I MUST HAVE been thirteen when I first read the book, a first edition hardback given to me by my father. The year was 1960, and I was ripe for an adventure story—three Southern children about my age, spending idyllic summers in the delicious, seductive fear of Boo Radley. My father, I think, saw other things. He was an Alabama judge possessing some of the same qualities as Atticus Finch, a quiet and unobtrusive understanding that occasionally a person is compelled to take a stand, despite a powerful preference to the contrary.

In addition to that, my father was proud that the author of *To Kill a Mockingbird* came from Monroe County, Alabama. That was where his own family had put down roots, making the trek from South Carolina to a place on the bluffs of the Alabama River. It was 1832, and those were dangerous times in Alabama. President Andrew Jackson had decreed that all Indians east of the Mississippi River be removed to Oklahoma, and as the Creeks who lived in Lower Alabama began their mournful Trail of Tears, there were assorted skirmishes with renegade bands.

The Gaillards, however, made their journey safely enough, and by the early years of the twentieth century were living in the village of Purdue Hill, just a few miles from Harper Lee's home. My father, like Dill in *To Kill a Mockingbird*, spent his boyhood summers there, sharing a favored swimming hole with the snakes, blissfully convinced that a moccasin would drown if it tried to bite a young boy in the water. My father's stories, as well as my own from an active childhood, blended easily with those of Harper Lee, and the adventures of Jem and Scout and Dill were as real to me as if I had been there.

But I think I sensed even then a deeper resonance for the members of my family. The faded aristocracy of the Finches, their indifference to money, and their graceful stewardship of prominence could have described the Gaillards just as well. There was, of course, a darker underside to the story—one that divided my family, as it did many others, when *To Kill a Mockingbird* first appeared. Though the novel was set in the 1930s, the issues it raised were still unresolved.

Harper Lee was a child when the backdrop of *Mockingbird* came into focus. She was luckier than some, shielded by the relative prosperity of her family, but she had to know even so that Alabama in the '30s was a desperate place—"a world coming apart," in the words of historian Wayne Flynt. The Depression landed hard on the rural parts of the state, so much so that when the great American writer James Agee set out to discover the face of Southern poverty, he came to Hale County in the Alabama Black Belt.

In his iconic book, *Let Us Now Praise Famous Men*, Agee entered the lives of white sharecroppers and offered a glimpse of grimness made even more vivid by the accompanying photographs of Walker Evans. Through Evans's lens—and the haunted eyes of his subjects—we could see the pain, the battered dignity and despair that we later encountered in the Cunninghams and Ewells of *To Kill a Mockingbird*.

But among the real families of Harper Lee's childhood, life was defined by more than the grinding misery of being poor. There was also the desperate issue of race. In the 1930s, as hard times amplified the tension, a rash of lynching and racial violence spread from the Black Belt all the way to Birmingham. On July 4, 1930, when Lee was only four years old, there was a startling case in the Sumter County town of Emelle, just a few miles northwest of Monroeville. A sharecropper by the name of Tom Robertson—a name, of course, only one syllable removed from the black hero of *To Kill a Mockingbird*—had argued with a white storekeeper about the price of a battery. On Independence Day, a mob appeared outside his cabin, and in self-defense Robertson opened fire with his shotgun.

Somehow, in the raging battle that followed, Robertson managed to escape. But four members of his family were lynched, and Robertson himself was captured two months later. On January 2, 1931, he died in the Alabama electric chair.

If it was a terrifying moment in southern Alabama, it was quickly overshadowed by events further north. In the town of Scottsboro near the Tennessee line, one of the most celebrated cases in Alabama history became a topic of conversation all over the state, and certainly in the home of young Harper Lee. On March 25, 1931, barely three months after the execution of Tom Robertson, a posse of whites arrested nine black hoboes on a freight train passing through the town of Paint Rock. Initially, the Negroes were wanted for assault—for fighting with a group of white boys on the train—but when the engine pulled into the Paint Rock station, two white women emerged from a boxcar and announced to the posse that they had been raped.

The doctors who examined the women weren't convinced. Victoria Price and Ruby Bates were neither battered nor bloody, as they should have been if they had been attacked by nine young men; and though there was evidence of sexual intercourse, the doctors found no vaginal tearing and no living sperm—strange if the rape had happened less than two hours earlier, as Bates and Price both insisted that it had. When one of the physicians, Dr. Marvin Lynch, suggested to the women that they were lying, he reported later that they simply laughed.

Nevertheless, the doomed defendants were hauled off to jail, the nearest of which was in the town of Scottsboro. As newspapers around Alabama trumpeted the story of "Nine Black Fiends," only the heroism of the local sheriff managed to keep a lynch mob at bay.

The trial that followed was quick and efficient. All nine defendants were convicted of rape, and eight were sentenced to death. Only Roy Wright, barely thirteen, was spared because of his tender years. On appeal, however, the U.S. Supreme Court overturned the conviction, ruling that "the Scottsboro Boys," as they were by then known, had been denied adequate legal representation. The drunken real estate attorney assigned to their defense, who had met his clients on the morning of the trial, offered no closing arguments in their behalf.

But if the original trial had been a caricature of Southern justice, the next one was not. It landed on the docket of Judge James Horton, who could well have been the model for Atticus Finch. To lawyers, juries, and even to defendants who came through his court, Horton was known for his informality and fairness, his commitment to equality in the eyes of the law. Like most white Alabamians, he entered the trial believing that the Scottsboro Boys were guilty. But as the testimony unfolded, he began to have his doubts.

Victoria Price, the Boys' chief accuser, struck him as shrill and evasive on the stand, but even more telling was the testimony of Dr. R. R. Bridges, one of the two physicians. Bridges testified that the sperm he found in Mrs. Price were "non-motile," which was nearly impossible if she had just been raped. And then came a decisive, off-the-record moment. During a break in the trial, the other doctor, Marvin Lynch, asked to speak to the judge in private. In the men's room, with the court bailiff standing guard near the door, Lynch told Horton that in his opinion there had been no rape. The medical evidence was simply not there.

The judge, who had spent a year in medical school before he entered the study of law, understood the importance of that kind of evidence. He urged Lynch to take the witness stand, but decided not to compel his testimony. He knew it could ruin the young doctor's career. But when the jury came in with a verdict of guilty, Horton decided he had to overturn it. Though it was within the power of a judge to do so, it was not a step to be taken lightly. For one thing, Horton believed in juries, believed in the ability of men duly sworn (all of them white, in those days) to deliver the most impartial verdict that they could. But he also knew that passions inflamed by the issue of race could lead them astray—and this, he concluded, was one of those times.

On June 22, 1933, citing contradictions in Price's testimony and the medical evidence casting doubt on the crime, Horton issued a ruling that stunned and enraged many white Alabamians:

"Deliberate injustice is more fatal to the one who imposes it than to the one on whom it is imposed," he declared. "The victim may die quickly and his suffering cease, but the teachings of Christianity and the uniform lesson of all history illustrate without exception that its perpetrators not only pay the penalty themselves, but their children through endless generations . . .

"It is therefore ordered and adjudged by the Court . . . that the verdict of the jury in this case and the judgment of the Court sentencing this defendant to death be set aside and that a new trial is hereby ordered."

Horton understood as he said it that his political career had come to an end. He would never be reelected as judge. But he also knew that even in Alabama, there were people who would understand what he did. And indeed there were. The members of the bar in his hometown of Athens wrote him a letter, signed by every lawyer in the town, declaring him to be "a judge of unimpeachable character and integrity."

The lawyers may not have put it this way, but on some level they must have regarded the judge as an archetype of Southern manhood. He had never wanted the Scottsboro case, never sought the fame or notoriety that it brought him. But when duty called, he remembered the Latin teachings of his mother: "*Justitia fiat coelum ruat*—Let justice be done though the Heavens may fall."

All of this made sense to Harper Lee. Coming of age at the time of the Scottsboro case, she understood the passions of her place, as well as the strength it took to resist them. And she thought she saw some of that strength in her father.

A. C. Lee, like Atticus Finch, was a pillar of the community in which he lived. In 1926, he was elected by the citizens of Monroeville to serve them in the state legislature, and as a lawyer and local newspaper editor, he was widely regarded by his friends and neighbors as a man of integrity. One of Harper Lee's biographers, Charles J. Shields, argues persuasively that Mr. Lee almost certainly played a role in the case of Walter Lett, a black man convicted of rape in Monroe County.

Since Lett's accuser was a white woman, nobody was surprised by the guilty verdict, or the sentence of death in the electric chair. But before the sentence could be carried out, on May 11, 1934, some of Monroeville's leading citizens, apparently including Lee, petitioned the governor on Lett's behalf. There was doubt, they said, about his guilt, for it was not uncommon for some white women—particularly those of a certain class—to cry rape in defense of their own reputations.

At the urging of such upright citizens, the governor commuted Lett's sentence to life in prison, but Lett by then had been driven insane. His cell in Alabama's Kilby Prison was only a few feet from the electric chair, and he had heard the sounds of other executions—the rush of the current, the screams of the dying—and he had simply snapped. "He now lies in a state of catalepsy," wrote the prison physician at Kilby, "and demonstrates fairly definite features of schizophrenia."

On July 30, 1934, Lett was moved to the Searcy Hospital for the Insane, an all-black facility in Mt. Vernon, Alabama, where he died three years later of tuberculosis.

It is impossible to say—and Harper Lee never has—exactly which pieces of this troubled history served as a model for *To Kill a Mockingbird*. Certainly, it's true that the Scottsboro case was more complex than the story of Atticus Finch and Tom Robinson. In Scottsboro, there were nine defendants, multiple appeals and stays of execution, four paroles, four dropped charges, and a daring escape. None of that happens in Harper Lee's story. But there *was* the inspirational story of Judge Horton, and the obstreperous example of Victoria Price—her dogged evasions on the witness stand and the wounded defiance that Mayella Ewell would exhibit in the novel.

More broadly, there was also the fact, as Miss Lee said later, that the Scottsboro case "will more than do as an example . . . of deep-South attitudes on race." But such examples abounded in the 1930s, many of them close to Harper Lee's home, and for a writer with an eye as keen as hers the leap was really not very large to the characters that began to take shape in her novel.

The transitions, however, did not come easily. Many readers were startled to learn later on, given the grace and certainty of her prose, that Miss Lee had struggled with her story for years. In his unauthorized biography, *Mockingbird*, Charles Shields offers a dramatic account of her writing—a young author living in a coldwater flat, working with her editor, Tay Hohoff, month after month, draft after draft, becoming so frustrated that at one point she threw her manuscript out the window. Fortunately, she thought better of it and retrieved the pages from the Manhattan snow.

But little by little, the narrative finally took on a shape, and the end result was one of the greatest triumphs in American letters. Miss Lee was thirty-four years old on July 11, 1960, when her novel was released to international acclaim. It was an immediate best seller for J. B. Lippincott & Co., won the Pulitzer Prize the following year, and a half century later, had sold an astonishing thirty million copies.

All of which raises the question of *why*. What was it about this particular book that touched the hearts of so many people? And why does it remain, after all this time, as popular as on the day of its release?

Every reader has his or her own answer, but I was struck first of all by the *voice*. Even as a boy, when I first read the book, I was captivated by the *telling* of the story—the sense almost of a double narrator, of a woman looking back on her childhood days with the wit and wisdom such perspective might imply; but also of a tomboy child caught entirely in the moment she was living. It struck me as quite a literary feat, for here was young Scout describing the house where Boo Radley lived, or the scene at the Maycomb County Jail, or the petty torments of certain members of her family.

Aunt Alexandra was fanatical on the subject of my attire. I could not possibly hope to be a lady if I wore breeches; when I said I could do nothing in a dress, she said I wasn't supposed to be doing things that required pants. Aunt Alexandra's vision of my deportment involved playing with small stoves, tea sets, and wearing the Add-A-Pearl necklace she gave me when I was born; furthermore, I should be a ray of sunshine in my father's lonely life. I suggested that one could be a ray of sunshine in pants just as well, but Aunty said that one had to behave like a sunbeam, that I was born good but had grown progressively worse every year. She hurt my feelings and set my teeth permanently on edge, but when I asked Atticus about it, he said there were already enough sunbeams in the family and to go on about my business, he didn't mind me much the way I was.

Every time I've ever read the story—and the count by now is closing in on a dozen—I've been struck by the singularity of that voice, the distinctiveness in the writing itself, that among other things should have put to rest the odd speculation that Truman Capote actually wrote Lee's book. It is true that Capote was the model for Dill, and true also that he read a draft of the novel and made suggestions on how to improve it. But the irony and wry humor that give an edge to the story, tempering its generosity of spirit, are pure Harper Lee. All of her letters, all the testimonials of her friends, confirm the originality of her voice, her view of the world that shines so brilliantly from the pages.

This is not Mayberry that she has created. Maycomb, Alabama, is a warts-and-all village full of characters familiar to us all. My own Aunt

Alexandra, for example, was a family elder whom I loved very much, a prim school teacher who did her job well and spent her spare time marveling at the heroism of her family. In my aunt's telling, Southern history would not have been the same without the Gaillards, and that glorious history was marred only by injury inflicted from the North. She had little patience with critics of the South, especially those who should have known better, and in that category she most emphatically included Harper Lee.

"I can't believe you are reading this book," she informed me when I was thirteen. When I asked her why, she replied in a way that ended our discussion, "It reads like it could have been written by a child."

Much later, of course, I came to understand that it was not Lee's style that offended my aunt, for she, in fact, had never read the book. Like many Southerners, she was driven instead by a ferocious belief in the rectitude of white supremacy, and the article of faith that went along with it—that the South was never wrong, only misunderstood. It is easy to forget, from the vantage point of today, that when *To Kill a Mockingbird* first appeared, a majority of white Southerners refused to concede its most basic point. They didn't want to hear about racial injustice, or our whispered history of oppression and violence, no matter how gently that story was told.

And so it was that Atticus Finch became a kind of prophet, a teller of truth in his own native land. Later generations may have found him paternal, or at least unremarkable in his racial understandings. Nevertheless, it was a memorable moment—made more so by Gregory Peck's performance in the movie—when Atticus stood before Tom Robinson's jury and proclaimed a truth that would seem unassailable:

. . . there is one way in this country in which all men are created equal— there is one human institution that makes a pauper the equal of a Rockefeller,

the stupid man the equal of an Einstein, and the ignorant man the equal of any college president. That institution, gentlemen, is a court. It can be the Supreme Court of the United States or the humblest J.P. court in the land, or this honorable court which you serve. Our courts have their faults, as does any human institution, but in this country our courts are the great levelers, and in our courts all men are created equal.

The problem, of course, as Harper Lee's readers understood very well, sometimes much to their own discomfort, was that there had *never* been a time or a place in the South in which all men were created equal. Nor did most people want there to be.

Miss Lee was not the first to make that point; she was, in fact, only the latest in a line of women writers who compelled a more honest look at their place. It was a literary tradition, you could argue, that began to take shape in 1940 and became in the course of the next twenty years a force too powerful to be dismissed.

II

In the dog days of August 1940, the great black author, Richard Wright, published a book review in the *New Republic*. In it he registered his frank astonishment at the achievement of a young writer named Carson McCullers. He was full of praise for McCullers's first novel, *The Heart Is a Lonely Hunter*, comparing it favorably to Hemingway and Faulkner, and marveling at the fact that the writer was only twenty-three years old. But there was something he found even more surprising than McCullers's tender age.

"To me," said Wright, "the most impressive aspect of *The Heart Is a Lonely Hunter* is the astonishing humanity that enables a white writer, for the first time in Southern fiction, to handle Negro characters with as much ease and justice as those of her own race. This cannot be accounted for stylistically or politically; it seems to stem from an attitude toward life which enables Miss McCullers to rise above the pressures of her environment and embrace white and black humanity in one sweep of apprehension and tenderness."

The Negro character that McCullers created was Dr. Benedict Copeland, a proud and fiercely intellectual man who hated the injustice he saw all around him. He found white people to be full of condescension, a "quiet insolence," he often called it, and his despair grew deeper as he saw his own children drift through the aimlessness of Negro life. But Copeland was not the only desperate soul in the Southern mill town of McCullers's creation. There were also a deaf-mute, a lonely young girl, and an alcoholic white man, who raged against capitalism and greed and flirted with the theories of Karl Marx.

What impressed Richard Wright as he read the story was not only McCullers's concern for social justice—her quiet explorations of racism and poverty—but also her color-blind empathy for the people of the South. And the question he raised between the lines of his review was whether this was merely an aberration, or whether it might be a beacon of hope. The answer came quickly from two other writers.

First, in 1941, a young Mississippian named Eudora Welty published her first collection of short stories, a volume entitled *A Curtain of Green*. The closing story was "A Worn Path," a tale so exquisitely beautiful in its telling that the prose alone left many people speechless.

She wore a dark striped dress reaching down to her shoe tops, and an equally long apron of bleached sugar sacks, with a full pocket: all neat and tidy, but every time she took a step she might have fallen over her shoelaces, which dragged from her unlaced shoes. She looked straight ahead. Her eyes were blue with age. Her skin had a pattern all its own of numberless branching wrinkles . . . as though a whole little tree stood in the middle of her forehead, but a golden color ran underneath, and the two knobs of her cheeks were illumined by a yellow burning under the dark. Under the red rag her hair came down on her neck in the frailest of ringlets, still black, and with an odor like copper.

The heroine of this eight-page epic is an ancient African American woman on a journey she has made many times. Phoenix Jackson, as the old woman is known, has a little grandson who has swallowed lye, and month after month when his throat swells shut, she follows a torturous path into town, stoic in the face of alligators, dogs, and contemptuous white people, driven by her patient love of a child.

As many critics have noted through the years, this was not a political tale Miss Welty was telling, not specifically racial in its intent. (That would come later in her long and distinguished career when she tried, for example, in one of her stories to enter the mind of a racist assassin.) But at the time it was published in 1941, "A Worn Path" had a powerful effect, for not only was the central character a Negro, she was a woman who carried herself with such courage that the whites she encountered seemed petty and small.

Such was Welty's affirmation of humanity.

But for me the most impressive of the new women writers—the most unforgettable when I came upon her work in the 1960s—was Lillian Smith, a native Floridian who spent much of her life in Georgia and came from an upper-middle-class family. When I read her book, *Killers of the Dream*, a collection of essays published in 1949, it occurred to me that she might go down as the bravest Southern writer of all time. Certainly, there has never been one more bold.

Smith's first taste of notoriety had come with the publication of her novel, *Strange Fruit*, a story of interracial love which took its title from a Billie Holiday song. Published in 1944, the novel became a national best seller, though it was banned for a time in Massachusetts because of its explicit sexuality. But it was *Killers of the Dream* that sealed Smith's fate as a lightning rod of Southern controversy. There had simply never been a book—certainly not one by a white Southern author—that confronted so directly the prevailing way of life in the South.

Smith's target was segregation itself, not only racial violence or the desperate excesses of the Ku Klux Klan, but the very foundation of Southern society. As her book makes clear, her sense of the absurdity of Jim Crow began to take shape when she was a child. She had overheard her parents talking in whispers. Not far away, a little white-skinned girl was living with Negroes, a scandalous thing in a small Southern town, and many of the neighbors began to speculate that maybe the child had been kidnapped. Against the protests of the black foster family, the little girl was seized by the local authorities and brought to live with Lillian and her family in a rambling farmhouse, full of laughing children, with a garden out back and wide open fields in which to play.

For a few happy weeks, Lillian took delight in this new and sweet-tempered younger sister, who seemed, in turn, to be astonished at her own good fortune. But then one day, a call came in from a Negro orphanage. "There was a meeting at our house," Smith explained in *Killers of the Dream.* "Many whispers. All afternoon the ladies went in and out of our house talking to Mother in tones too low for children to hear. As they passed us at play, they looked at Janie and quickly looked away again, though a few stopped and stared at her as if they could not tear their eyes from her face."

What the ladies of the community had learned was that Janie, despite the fact that her skin was white, was the orphaned child of a

Negro family. She was sent back immediately to colored town—to the foster family from whom she was seized—and Lillian and her siblings were told never to speak of the incident again. "You're too young to understand," Smith remembers her mother saying, in a command that seemed both brittle and rigid. "And don't ask me ever again about this!"

For more than thirty years the experience was wiped out of my memory. But that night, and the weeks it was tied to, worked its way like a splinter, bit by bit, down to the hurt places in my memory and festered there. And as I grew older, as more experiences collected around that faithless time, as memories of earlier, more profound hurts crept closer, drawn to that night as if to a magnet, I began to know that people who talked of love and children did not mean it. That is a hard thing for a child to learn. I still admired my parents, there was so much that was strong and vital and sane and good about them and I never forgot this . . . Yet in my heart they were under suspicion . . . I was shamed by their failure and frightened, for I felt they were no longer as powerful as I had thought. There was something Out There that was stronger than they and I could not bear to believe it . . .

As I read that story in *Killers of the Dream*, I remember thinking that even as late as my own generation, every Southern child probably had some similar experience, some startling moment of racial revelation that may or may not have touched the heart. I certainly did. Though the memory, like Smith's, had been submerged, there was a day in the early 1950s when I was maybe five years old that my mother and I, along with another member of our family, went to visit a servant who had been taken ill. This elderly African American woman lived in a cabin on the edge of Mobile; only two rooms, as I remember it now, with very little paint and no electricity or indoor plumbing.

Children played on the dusty lane leading to similar houses nearby, and I remember being struck, though I was far too young to express it at the time, by the terrible bleakness that must cripple their lives.

"Aren't these children unhappy?" I remember asking. And my mother, a lovely and kindhearted Southern woman, who would one day emerge as a racial liberal, did her best to stammer out a reply.

"They are not like we are," she said.

Reading *Killers of the Dream*, I felt the memory come flooding back, giving added force to Smith's explanation of how it all came to be. As she understood it, the oppressions of slavery, sharecropping, and segregation compelled Southern whites, who wanted to regard themselves as decent, to regard their African American neighbors as somehow less than human. Otherwise, how could they explain the appalling conditions they saw all around?

That was what it came down to, and from the tangled roots of that belief, which twined back deep into Southern history, came a complex set of notions that produced a society of moral cripples. That was how Smith saw it, and in her unrelenting critique she also argued that our very ability to think was compromised in a fundamental way, for we were compelled every day of our lives to rationalize things that our hearts inevitably understood to be absurd.

I do not remember how or when but by the time I had learned that God is love, that Jesus is His Son and came to give us more abundant life, that all men are brothers with a common Father, I also knew that I was better than a Negro, that all black folks have their place and must be kept in it, that sex has its place and must be kept in it, that a terrifying disaster would befall the South if ever I treated a Negro as my social equal and as terrifying a disaster would befall my family if ever I were to have a baby outside of marriage . . . I learned it the way all of my Southern people learn it: by closing door after door until one's mind and heart and conscience are blocked off from each other and from reality.

Reading *Killers of the Dream* in the 1960s, I could not imagine how, in 1949, Lillian Smith found the courage to write it, or why the retributions she faced were not more extreme. Perhaps it was because she had that gift—that ability of Southern writers from Robert Penn Warren to Pat Conroy, Eudora Welty to Willie Morris and Rick Bragg—to create such beauty with the language itself. For even as her poetry helped her to dig through the hardest, least appealing layers of the truth, still she was able to give sweet voice to the things about the South that she loved:

. . . jessamine crawling on fences and trees, giving out a wonder of yellow fragrance, bays blooming white and delicate down in the swamp, and water lilies fattening on green pond water, making you love the loneliness you hate, making you want to stay even as you feel you must leave or die.

III

Lillian Smith developed breast cancer in the 1950s. But even as she fought it, until death finally took her at the age of sixty-eight, she pursued her career as a writer and an activist. In 1955, she published a new book called *Now Is the Time*, urging compliance with the U.S. Supreme Court's *Brown* decision, and the following year she threw her support behind the Montgomery bus boycott. She soon became friendly with Dr. Martin Luther King Jr. and his wife, Coretta, and on the night of May 4, 1960, the Kings were driving her to Emory University Hospital in Atlanta, where Smith was undergoing cancer treatments. A policeman stopped them on the way, curious about this interracial group, and discovered that King, who had recently moved to Atlanta, still had an Alabama driver's license.

For this misdemeanor offense, King received a one-year suspended prison sentence, and the following fall, when he was arrested during an Atlanta sit-in, the judge revoked the suspension and ordered King to spend four months on a Georgia chain gang. He was led away from the courtroom in chains.

Hearing about these events, Senator John F. Kennedy, who was running for president, picked up the phone and called Coretta Scott King, asking if there was anything he could do. Within a few hours, the senator's brother, Robert Kennedy, made a private call to the judge in the case and persuaded him to release King on bail. Word quickly spread within the African American community, not only in Atlanta, but nationwide, and for his simple act of compassion John F. Kennedy became a hero. Black Americans, who had voted overwhelmingly Republican in 1956, voted for Kennedy in 1960 by the stunning margin of seventy percent to thirty percent.

Thus did Lillian Smith become a curious footnote to presidential history. But she is remembered, of course, for more than that, for hers was one of the strongest voices in a line of women writers—beginning with McCullers and Eudora Welty—who compelled a more honest look at the South. Flannery O'Connor followed quite importantly in the 1950s with her Southern Gothic characters and dissenting opinions on religion and race, and then Harper Lee. Each of these women, in her own way, left an important literary mark, and each had a powerful effect on the cultural and social history of the region.

There were important differences among them, of course. If Lillian Smith was intentionally political in much of her writing, the others were not. But all were caught inevitably in the current of the times. *To Kill a Mockingbird* appeared in 1960, the year of the first civil rights sit-ins, and the movie that followed premiered in Alabama at the time of the Birmingham demonstrations—the fire hoses and dogs, and a few months later the bombing of a church in the heart of the city, killing four children and creating a specter of deadly injustice. It was no surprise against such a backdrop that Atticus Finch would emerge as an iconic character, a repository of the sanity and fairness that many white Southerners believed—or hoped—lay dormant somehow in the heart of our place.

Maybe that is why of all the books by these great writers, *To Kill a Mockingbird* is the most beloved. For many of us, the most appealing thing about Atticus Finch was something profoundly simple and reassuring. He was one of us.

· 3 ·

Across the Divide

I

As AMERICA MADE its way through the racial crisis of the 1960s, a lot of us began to read black writers, trying to make sense out of what was going on. Some of the most fashionable —Eldridge Cleaver and Nikki Giovanni come to mind—were, in the words of Henry Louis Gates, "incandescent with racial rage." I think I had a feeling even then that their work was more catharsis than literature, but for me at least, that was not the case with Richard Wright. From the moment I opened his first book, a collection of short stories called *Uncle Tom's Children*, I was captivated by this Southern-born author whose life and writing had been shaped so profoundly by the terrible events of a troubled childhood.

He was born in Mississippi in 1908, the grandson of runaway slaves who had fought for the Union in the Civil War. Wright remembered his maternal grandfather, Richard Wilson, as a man of silent bitterness and rage. The old man, like others his age, had lived through what may have been the greatest disappointment ever inflicted on a generation of Americans. Having fled from slavery in 1865, he served three months in the Union Navy before the war was over and he was free. Like many former slaves, he expected to take his place as a citizen—to make a living, to vote, to worship in a church of his own choosing, perhaps to see his children educated—and for a while things seemed to be headed that way.

But sharecropping, the immediate heir to slavery in the South, offered little hope of economic gain, and within a few years whites began to reassert their power, using terror and intimidation to strip black people of the right to vote. Segregation laws soon followed and by the early years of the twentieth century—the years of Richard Wright's childhood—African Americans were trapped in a crippled imitation of freedom, subjected constantly to the whims of Southern whites.

"I never heard him speak of white people," Wright later wrote of his grandfather. "I think he hated them too much to talk of them."

For Wright, however, whites were not the source of his earliest misery, at least not directly, for he suffered instead from the terrifying dysfunctions of his own family. In his autobiography, *Black Boy*, he opens with a story of the time his mother nearly beat him to death. He was barely four years old when it happened, playing with his brother on a winter day, when he accidentally set fire to the house. In her horror and grief, his mother, Ella Wright, began to beat him with a switch, slashing again and again across his body until he finally passed out from the pain. Later he lapsed into fevers and chills, and a doctor who was called by the family said the boy's life was hanging in the balance.

Even after he finally recovered, he was left with an emotionally devastating thought. ". . . I was chastened," he wrote, "whenever I remembered that my mother had come close to killing me."

His childhood anguish continued from there, as the family moved from place to place through the South, and for many years he lived with the feeling that almost all of his relatives disliked him. And then came a newfound terror of whites. When Richard was eight, he and his mother went to live with an aunt in Elaine, Arkansas, a sawmill town where his uncle, Silas Hoskins, had established a profitable saloon for the black mill hands. Hoskins was a controversial figure, resented by whites for his success, and he slept with a pistol by his bed for protection.

One night he didn't come home from work, and the family learned that he had been killed—murdered by whites who had also threatened the members of his family. Richard's aunt and mother fled in panic, taking Richard with them, and the three of them hid for days in a rented room in the town of West Helena. There was never an investigation of the shooting, never a funeral, never a resolution of the terror. "Uncle Hoskins had simply been plucked from our midst," Wright would later recount in *Black Boy*, "and we, figuratively, had fallen on our faces to avoid looking into that white-hot face of terror that we knew loomed somewhere above us . . . Why had we not fought back, I asked my mother, and the fear that was in her made her slap me into silence."

For Wright, the only reprieve from the unrelenting agonies of his youth came from an unexpected source, his discovery of books. He had always loved to read in school, but the breakthrough came when he was eighteen and living in Memphis. One morning, as he often did, he bought a copy of the *Memphis Commercial Appeal*, and thumbing through the pages, he came to an editorial denouncing H. L. Mencken, the American satirist, for his unkind words about the South. Intrigued, Wright made his way to the public library—an all-white facility in 1926—and presented the librarian with a note he had written himself: *Madame: Will you please let this nigger boy have some books by H. L. Mencken?* Wright ended the note with the forged signature of a white man, and the librarian, though dubious, gave him two of Mencken's titles, *Prejudices* and *A Book of Prefaces.*

That night in his room Wright found himself reading until almost dawn, astonished by the power of Mencken's prose. "I was jarred and shocked by the style," he remembered, "the clear, clean sweeping sentences. Why did he write like that? And how did one write like that? I pictured the man as a raging demon, slashing with his pen . . . He was using words as a weapon, using them as one would use a club. Could words be weapons? Well, yes, for here they were. Then, maybe, perhaps, I could use them as weapons? No. It frightened me. I read on and what amazed me was not what he said, but how on earth anybody had the courage to say it."

Other trips to the library quickly followed, for Mencken, in his criticism, introduced Wright to authors whose names he had never even heard: Sinclair Lewis, Upton Sinclair, Stephen Crane, Dostoevsky, Balzac, Tolstoy, T. S. Eliot. "Reading was like a drug, a dope," Wright recalled, and it awakened something deep inside. "I had once tried to write, had once reveled in feeling, had let my crude imagination roam, but the impulse to dream had been slowly beaten out of me by experience. Now it surged up again and I hungered for books, new ways of looking and seeing. It was not a matter of believing or disbelieving what I read, but of feeling something new, of being affected by something that made the look of the world different."

I had learned these things about Richard Wright, had followed his journey toward becoming a writer, by reading *Black Boy*. But it was not my introduction to him. That came in the form of *Uncle Tom's Children*, his book of short stories published in 1938, a slash-and-burn portrayal of the South, written after he had moved to the North. The fury of the prose was gripping in itself—"words as weapons" describing in graphic, unforgettable terms the racial cruelties he had seen growing up.

The first story is the one most people remember. "Big Boy Leaves Home" contains, in the course of its forty-five pages, one of the most horrifying scenes in American fiction—a black boy lynched, tarred and feathered and burned alive, for his unintended role in the killing of a white man. Another of his friends being hunted by the mob is forced to hide in a cave nearby, unable to do anything but watch.

The scream came again. Big Boy trembled and looked. The mob was running down the slopes, leaving the fire clear. Then he saw a writhing white mass cradled in yellow flame, and heard screams, one on top of the other, each shriller and shorter than the last.

It is a scene so vivid, so elemental in its violence that even black writers like Zora Neale Hurston were appalled—startled by the lack of redemption in the story. But Wright believed he was telling the truth, forcing the country to confront, perhaps in a way that it never had, the reality of violence and lynching in the South.

He also knew there was more than savagery in his brutal word pictures.

In the last of the four novellas in the book, a story that he called "Bright and Morning Star," he sketched an aching, fully realized portrait of Sue, a black woman struggling to understand the world.

Long hours of scrubbing floors for a few cents a day had taught her who Jesus was, what a great boon it was to cling to Him, to be like Him and suffer without a mumbling word. She had poured the yearning of her life into the songs, feeling buoyed with a faith beyond this world. The figure of the Man nailed in agony to the Cross, His burial in a cold grave, His transfigured Resurrection, His being breath and clay, God and Man—all had focused her feelings upon an imagery which had swept her life into a wondrous vision.

But against that faith and her love of old hymns loomed the terrible reality of the world, and she had two sons who were ready to fight, ready to struggle in the here and now for the justice that lay in a different kind of vision. Lacking other allies, her boys had joined the Communist party, a decision more common in the 1930s than many people remember, and they dreamed of a day when poor whites and blacks would come together against a common foe. Slowly, inevitably, the dream had become their mother's as well, and she was astonished at the way it made her feel.

And day by day her sons had ripped from her startled eyes her old vision, and image by image had given her a new one, different, but great and strong enough to fling her into the light of another grace. The wrongs and sufferings of black men had taken the place of Him nailed to the Cross; the meager beginnings of the party had become another Resurrection; and the hate of those who would destroy her new faith had quickened in her a hunger to feel how deeply her new strength went.

She knew they might pay a terrible price, but like her sons she was willing to pay it, for she knew it would be the cost of their faith.

As I read these dark and disturbing stories, written with such improbable beauty, I was struck by the power of the truth they contained.

I had already read enough history to know that the grim statistics were on Wright's side. As historian Joel Williamson has noted, during a period beginning in 1889 and lasting through the end of World War II, nearly four thousand blacks were lynched in America, mostly in the South. This was more than one a week for nearly sixty years, and these were not just random murders, but grisly, stylized executions, most often carried out by a mob.

"There was indeed," Williamson wrote, "something new and horribly palpable on the earth. It was signalized by the mob, the rushing, swelling fury of a mass of struggling men, the bloody and mangled bodies, and the smell of burning flesh."

In *Uncle Tom's Children*, Wright had given that reality a face, but now the questions loomed unanswered. What were we to do with that legacy? Was it possible for America to deal with it at all?

II

For Richard Wright, the answer was no. Or at least that seemed to be his verdict when he moved to Paris in 1946 and entered the American expatriate community. He soon became friends with the existentialist authors Albert Camus and Jean Paul Sartre, and with a young American writer, James Baldwin, who had recently arrived in Paris from Harlem. Baldwin shared with Wright a literary quest to come to terms with his blackness, and all the implications that it held.

Baldwin was born in 1924, and his own life story, though set initially in a different place, held similar memories of family dysfunction. Raised in Harlem, Baldwin never knew his biological father, but his stepfather, David Baldwin, was a cruel, bombastic tyrant of a man who wrapped his terrible temper in piety. He worked for his daily wages in a factory, but he also served as a part-time preacher, and whatever his gifts may have been in the pulpit, his children cowered in the face of his rage.

On the day he died, August 2, 1943, a race riot broke out in Harlem, and in Baldwin's first book of essays, *Notes of a Native Son*, he remembered the funeral procession.

We drove my father to the graveyard through a wilderness of smashed plate glass . . . He had lived and died in intolerable bitterness of spirit and it frightened me, as we drove him through those unquiet, ruined streets, to see how powerful and overflowing this bitterness could be and to realize that it was now mine.

Again and again in the course of his writings, Baldwin made clear his own understanding that racism in America—and the crippled humanity that went along with it—was not a problem confined to the South. His first encounter with segregation had come when he was in his late teens and went to work in a defense plant in New Jersey. The restaurants nearby refused to serve him, and his supervisors and white co-workers all seemed to hate him for his self-esteem—his refusal, simply, to carry himself with any kind of deference.

For all his life, he had sensed his father's hatred of whites, but his father seemed to hate everybody, or at least to mistrust them, and in the schools that Baldwin attended (and in which he had flourished, largely because of his gift with the language) he had found white teachers who were genuinely kind. But now, he discovered, there was a new kind of tension in the streets of Harlem, for the nation had now entered World War II and black soldiers who had gone to fight for their country wrote home about the indignities they encountered—not at the hands of Germans or Japanese, but from fellow soldiers who were white.

Many of these indignities occurred in the South, where the black recruits had gone for basic training. But then came the night in 1943 when much of Harlem exploded in rage. It began with an argument between a black soldier and a white policeman, which ended with the soldier being shot. In the violence that followed, there was massive looting of white-owned stores, and Baldwin saw how destructive such bitterness could be.

And yet he had to admit that he felt it. Sorting through his emotions in the years that followed, he found himself writing from his Paris sanctuary: "I was forced to admit something I had always hidden from myself, which the American Negro has had to hide from himself as the price of his public progress: that I hated and feared white people. This did not mean that I loved black people; on the contrary, I despised them, possibly because they had failed to produce Rembrandt. In effect, I hated and feared the world."

I had read some of these words as a college student in the 1960s. But my first real dive into Baldwin's work came sometime early in the 1970s. I discovered an article in *Harper's* magazine, published in 1958, recounting his first visit to the South. As it happened, he had come to Charlotte, North Carolina, the city where I was working as a journalist, and the story he had come to write about—the desegregation of Charlotte's public schools—was the one I was covering, more than a decade after it began.

In September 1957, four teenagers had broken the color barrier in the city, and Baldwin read about it in a Paris newspaper. There was a photograph that went with the story, the image of a girl who was maybe fifteen making her way through a mob of white students. She seemed so alone in her prim, checked dress with a bow at the collar, her head erect, no trace of fear in her round, pretty eyes. "It filled me with both hatred and pity," Baldwin wrote in *Harper's*, "and it made me ashamed. Some one of us should have been there with her!"

He decided immediately that he would leave his expatriate friends in Paris and travel to the American South, a place that had always filled him with dread. He remembered later how he stared out the window of his plane and noticed the rust-red color of the soil. He couldn't suppress the thought, he said, "that this earth had acquired its color from the blood that had dripped down from these trees. My mind was filled with the image of a black man, younger than I, perhaps, or my own age, hanging from a tree, while white men watched him and cut out his sex with a knife . . . The southern landscape—the trees, the silence, the liquid heat, and the fact that one always seems to be traveling great distances—seems designed for violence, seems, almost, to demand it. What passions cannot be unleashed on a southern night!"

In the end, however, Baldwin found something on his journey he had not been expecting—Southern white people who, even in 1957, were grappling honestly with the changes beginning to take place around them. On his stop in Charlotte, he met Ed Sanders, principal of the city's Central High School, where one of the black teenagers had been assigned. "He explained to me, with difficulty," Baldwin wrote, "that desegregation was contrary to everything he'd ever seen or believed. He'd never dreamed of a mingling of the races; had never lived that way himself and didn't suppose he ever would . . . The eyes came to life then, or a veil fell, and I found myself staring at a man in anguish. The eyes were full of pain and bewilderment . . . It is not an easy thing to be forced to reexamine a way of life and to speculate, in a personal way, on the general injustice."

As it happened, by the time I read Baldwin's article in *Harper's*, I had come to know Ed Sanders well; knew him as a good and decent man who had walked side by side through the mob with the first black student who came to his school, and had dedicated much of his career to the cause of integration. I asked him sometime early in the 1970s if he remembered Baldwin's visit in 1957.

Oh, yes, he said, he remembered it well. He had been deeply impressed by this earnest young writer from New York City, who had come to Charlotte by way of Paris. "He was not critical of us," said Sanders. "He was just asking a whole lot of questions." Certainly, it was clear enough to Sanders that Baldwin was there to document injustice, but he also seemed to be eager to learn, perhaps to record those glimmers of decency that might matter in the struggle within his own heart.

That, at least, was our speculation when Sanders and I talked about the encounter, and it was soon after that that I picked up a copy of *The Fire Next Time*. In this extended essay, published in 1963, Baldwin wrestled with the lure of black separatism, which was gaining momentum in the 1960s, as powerful leaders such as Malcolm X gave voice to the rage in the nation's ghettoes. It was an anger that Baldwin understood very well.

The brutality with which Negroes are treated in this country simply cannot be overstated, however unwilling white men may be to hear it. In the beginning—and neither can this be overstated—a Negro just cannot believe that white people are treating him as they do; he does not know what he has done to merit it. And when he realizes that the treatment accorded him has nothing to do with anything he has done, that the attempt of white people to destroy him—for that is what it is—is utterly gratuitous, it is not hard for him to think of white people as devils.

It seemed to me as I read both Baldwin and Wright that I was seeing the poetry and evolution of black rage. For here was Wright in the 1930s, armed with the terrible weapon of his words, flinging the truth at white America, hoping for nothing except to be heard. But now, barely more than twenty years later, James Baldwin improbably was hoping for more. He understood the toll of his country's racism, in the South, certainly, but also in the North. And yet he had seen certain things along the way—a young black girl in Charlotte, North Carolina, serene in the face of the white mob around her, and a white man, too, who later faced the same kind of mob, guiding a black student into his school. Perhaps neither one had wanted to be there, but each had come to a powerful understanding: that they were, inevitably, caught up together in the reluctant quest to build a better world.

For Baldwin in the end, neither black nor white could afford the luxury of anything less, for the price was likely to be measured in violence, and even worse, in a spirit-killing bitterness that affected us all. "We, the black and the white," he wrote, "deeply need each other . . . if we are really to become a nation." But the question, he wondered, was whether we would realize it in time. Writing in 1963, Baldwin was afraid that time was running out, as all Americans, black and white together, approached the prophecy of an old slave song:

God gave Noah the rainbow sign, No more water, the fire next time!

III

I think it was the artfulness of these warnings, the elegant language in pursuit of hard truth, that first attracted my attention. I was, after all, an aspiring writer myself, and I envied the talent of Baldwin and Wright. But it was also true that I was drawn to their subject matter as well, felt that their stories were somehow mine, for all of us—it seemed obvious to me—were caught in the great melodrama of race.

It is safe to say that many African Americans disagreed. The brilliant

Southern novelist William Styron was pilloried for his presumption in daring to write *The Confessions of Nat Turner*, a book, as it happened, that I deeply admired. And even a few journalists like myself, white writers who played it closer to the vest, were viewed as interlopers at best, trying to tell a story that we couldn't understand.

All of which makes me wish, looking back, that I had discovered Albert Murray much sooner. It was strange in many ways that I didn't, for he was a writer who came from my hometown. Born in Mobile in 1916, Murray grew up on the northern edge of the city, where a neighborhood of shotgun houses lay in the shadow of a black water swamp. Even as a boy, he sensed the hostility of the white world around him, but the message driven home by his elders—by the community that raised him—was that Southern racism was simply a given, a reality to be negotiated every day, but not an excuse for personal failure.

Boy, don't come telling me nothing about no old white folks. Boy, ain't nothing you can tell me about no white folks.

As Murray's writing makes clear, he was an avid reader by the time he finished high school, having been pushed to excel by his favorite teacher, Mister Baker. (That was the way he always wrote it, spelling the courtesy title in full as a gesture of gratitude and respect.) The teacher, Benjamin Baker, thought he saw something special in Murray, a rare intellect and hunger to learn, and both of them knew, without even having to say it aloud, that such gifts ultimately belonged to their community. Baker had studied the great black thinkers, from Frederick Douglass to Booker T. Washington and W. E. B. DuBois, and he shared with Murray his estimations of their legacy:

"Booker T. Washington sacrificed too much to expediency. Dr. DuBois

in his up-north bitterness spends too much time complaining. The youth of today must find the golden mean."

With such thoughts swimming in his eager young mind, Murray left Mobile for Tuskegee Institute, which was in those days, and remains today, a vibrant memorial to the vision of its founder. Booker Washington came to Tuskegee in 1881, teaching the first classes on July 4, and died in November 1915, the year before Albert Murray was born. But the Institute's most famous professor, George Washington Carver, was still on campus when Murray arrived, still working in his lab, still accessible to students who might seek his counsel. There were other teachers, too, who earned a place of legend in the minds of many students—and even those students, to Murray, were impressive. Perhaps the one he admired most was an upperclassman by the name of Ralph Ellison, a music major from Oklahoma, who would go on to write *Invisible Man*, a masterpiece of American letters, published in 1952.

In the years after college, the two became close friends, sharing a love of books, but also of music, especially jazz and the blues, where it seemed to Murray that the finest musicians anywhere in the country—people, for example, like his friend Duke Ellington—had the artist's gift for transforming sadness, for *riffing* on the lowdown feelings of life, and creating joy and beauty in their place. They were like an echo of the elders back home, people whose words and laughter and wisdom were not only their armor against a segregated world, but sounded to Murray almost like a song. And some years later, when he began to make his mark as a writer, he tried to find that music in his prose.

Sometimes a thin gray, ghost-whispering mid-winter drizzle would begin while you were still at school and not only would it settle in for the rest of

the afternoon but it would still be falling after dark as if it would continue
throughout the night . . . As nobody ever needed to tell me . . . it was one
of the very best of all good times to be where grown folks were talking . . .

Those were the first words I ever read by Murray, the opening lines
of a story in *Harper's*, and I thought as I made my way through the
pages that this was a writer who loved being black. I don't remember
dwelling on it at the time, but it seemed in 1969 when rage was the
stock and trade of black writers, that Murray was attuned to something
very different—to the strength and resilience, far more than the pain,
at the heart of black life.

And then for some reason, I simply moved on and didn't read him
again until I finally encountered, quite by accident, his memoir, *South
to a Very Old Place*. Published in 1971, it was the second of Murray's
dozen books, which included fiction, nonfiction and poetry written
over a period of more than thirty years. The memoir—still to me his
most fascinating work—helped to seal Murray's double-edged reputation as perhaps the ultimate black integrationist. But if that was the
pigeonhole du jour, it has to be said that with Murray it could be a
disconcerting truth.

"In Murray's hands," wrote Harvard author Henry Louis Gates,
"integration wasn't an act of accommodation but an act of introjec-
tion . . . perhaps the most breathtaking act of cultural chutzpah this
land has witnessed since Columbus blithely claimed it all for Isabella."

What Gates was saying was that Murray could meet white America
halfway precisely because he was secure in his blackness, in the depth of
a personal and cultural identity that was nurtured when he was growing up in Mobile. Thus, Murray would write about William Faulkner,
an author whose artistry he admired, and whose racial sensitivity was
more developed than most:

When William Faulkner declares as he did in the eulogy he delivered at her funeral that his black mammy was a "fount of authority over my conduct and of security for my physical welfare, and of active and constant affection and love," and that she was also "an active and constant precept for decent behavior, from her I learned to tell the truth, to refrain from waste, to be considerate of the weak and respectful of age," you don't doubt that he was deeply moved as he spoke or was moved again every time he remembered what he said, but being one of black mammy's taffy- and chocolate-colored boys you could not only tell him a few things, you could also ask him a hell of a lot of pretty embarrassing questions, beginning, for instance, with: "Damn, man, if the mammyness of blackness or the blackness of mammyness was so magnificent and of such crucial significance as you now claim, how come you let other white folks disrespect and segregate her like that? . . . Man, do you really think your reciprocation was adequate?

Throughout its 266 pages, *South to a Very Old Place* resonates with such observations. But there are also, delivered quite often when you least expect them, those flashes of generosity and acceptance that formed the other side of Murray's understanding. One of the most revealing scenes in the book was his description of a visit with Walker Percy, a Louisiana novelist living just north of New Orleans, whose debut best seller, *The Moviegoer*, was one of Murray's favorites. He discovered, as expected, that he and Percy shared a love of good writing—of Hemingway, Faulkner, and T. S. Eliot, of Flannery O'Connor and Robert Penn Warren. But in the early stages of their warm conversation, he couldn't help wondering if Percy might slip into unintended condescension. He was after all the favorite nephew of William Alexander Percy, a Southern writer from an earlier generation, whose plantation memoir, *Lanterns on the Levee*, was filled with declarations such as these:

I would say to the Negro: before demanding to be a white man socially and politically, learn to be a white man morally and intellectually—and to the white man, the black man is our brother, a younger brother, not adult, not disciplined, but tragic, pitiful, and lovable. Act as his brother and be patient.

Try as he might, Albert Murray could scarcely imagine a passage more offensive. But even with his antennae on high alert, he detected nothing like it from Walker Percy—no hidden agendas, no whiff of racial arrogance, just a pleasant companion on a Louisiana night. And then as the evening was drawing to a close, the two of them began to talk about trees. Did Percy know the difference, Murray wanted to know, between a mulberry bush and a mulberry tree? Because Murray had tried unsuccessfully to look it up and was unsure of the precise definition.

Percy was not sure either, but a week or so later an envelope arrived at Murray's apartment in Harlem. Inside were a leaf and a handwritten note: "Al, is this the leaf? If it is it's a Spanish mulberry—has a purple berry. Shelby was disappointed not to see you." As Murray understood, "Shelby" was a reference to Shelby Foote, the novelist turned historian and Civil War scholar who had been unable to make it to dinner that night. But perhaps the most striking thing about the note was how essentially unremarkable it was—simply a small and thoughtful gesture, directed unobtrusively from one friend to another.

For Murray the change was duly noted. Not that he waxed sentimental about it, but it was clearly the case that in one generation the Percy family had shed a major piece of Old South baggage. ". . . It is precisely," Murray later wrote, "Walker Percy's freedom from condescension that you are inclined to vouch for first of all."

IV

I have never met Albert Murray, much to my everlasting disappointment. But my friend Jay Lamar, a respected Alabama writer and editor, has gotten to know him well through the years. Murray, she has written, believes that race matters deeply in America, but so does the shared humanity of black and white. And it is, she explains, a humanity he discovered in "the territory of the blues"—that literal and metaphorical land he encountered as a boy growing up in Mobile, and as an artist who plied his trade in Harlem. Murray doesn't romanticize these communities. Indeed, says Lamar, these were the places where he first understood that "life is a lowdown dirty shame."

But in the existential gospel of Albert Murray, all of us share with the artists among us—particularly the great practitioners of the blues—the opportunity to find our meaning in the struggle and to transform ugliness into beauty. "We do not receive wisdom," Murray writes, "we must discover it for ourselves, after a journey through the wilderness that no one else can make for us, that no one can spare us, for our wisdom is the point of view from which we come at last to view the world."

And so it is that Murray, perhaps even more than Baldwin and Wright, is a writer whose work belongs to us all—who believes in the very depth of his soul that black identity and American identity are joined at the heart. But in praising Murray, I don't mean to denigrate the others—or for that matter any of their brilliant peers; not Ellison or Morrison, not Hurston or Hughes. For in the great complexity of our original sin, in struggling with what could—or should?—have been a fatal flaw, we were lucky enough to discover on the way the discomfort that came from reading their words.

· 4 ·

The Power of the Truth

FEATURING:

The Old Man and Lesser Mortals—Larry L. King

Radical Chic & Mau-Mauing the Flak Catchers—Tom Wolfe

The Unfinished Odyssey of Robert Kennedy—David Halberstam

ALSO, WILLIE MORRIS, JIMMY BRESLIN

I

IN APRIL 1971, I opened my copy of *Harper's* magazine, and thumbing through the pages I came upon an article by Larry L. King—not to be confused with Larry King, the gravelly voiced talk show host on CNN. Larry *L.* King was (and I suppose still is) a profane, flamboyant Texas roustabout, son of a dirt farmer, and by the early 1970s, one of the stars of literary journalism. I had read some of his earlier pieces, one of the most disturbing of which was a profile of Brother Dave Gardner, a comedian whose career had peaked in the 1950s with his manic, down-home monologues, a half-dozen of which had produced hit records.

But a little more than a decade later, when Larry L. King caught up with him at a comedy club on the outskirts of Charlotte—"Klan Country," according to a billboard just up the road—Gardner's act had degenerated into a bizarre and disjointed political rant. "Do y'all remember, dear hearts, when they awarded that Nobel Peace Prize to the late Dr. Junior on account of his efficiency in teaching our New Citizens to riot? Man, what's that Nobel cat doing giving a *peace* prize, after he done went and invented dynamite?"

"Then," wrote Larry King, "he hit them with the line that caused a sudden shocked silence, a line that even many of the Good Ole Boys deepest into the mysteries of their brown bags were not braced for, and it stunned them, caused gasps, a quick dark murder of laughter. Maybe the wild grin on his face, the sheer exuberance of his delivery, were as petrifying as the line itself: *"God, wasn't that a clean hit on Dr. Junior?"*

Even as a reader, I remember being stunned, reminded of that subterranean darkness that was still a part of the Southern heart and soul, at least in scattered corners of the countryside, among the hard-core patrons of those hard-liquor dives, where most of us would prefer not to go. But Larry King had been there, spending six days with Brother Dave, and marveling with every passing hour at the terrifying lunacy in which he took such delight.

After reading that story in *Harper's*, I have to say I was not quite prepared for King's contribution to the April issue. Entitled simply "The Old Man," it was a story about his father, one of the most tender and well-crafted pieces—then as now, perhaps the most touching magazine article—that I have ever read. This is how it began:

While we digested our suppers on The Old Man's front porch, his grand-

children chased fireflies in the summer dusk and, in turn, were playfully chased by neighborhood dogs. As always, The Old Man had carefully locked the collar of his workday khakis. He recalled favored horses and mules from his farming days, remembering their names and personalities though they had been thirty or forty years dead. I gave him a brief thumbnail sketch of William Faulkner— Mississippian, great writer, appreciator of the soil and good bourbon—before quoting what Faulkner had written of the mule: "He will draw a wagon or a plow but he will not run a race. He will not try to jump anything he does not indubitably know beforehand he can jump; he will not enter any place unless he knows of his own knowledge what is on the other side; he will work for you patiently for ten years for the chance to kick you once." The Old Man cackled in delight. "That feller sure knowed his mules," he said.

It was, I discovered, a lovely foreshadowing of what was to come: a story of two generations reaching out across the years, of a family divided by mutating values, but straining against time to cobble some new understanding. Clyde Clayton King, as The Old Man was known, had come to Texas in a covered wagon back in 1895, and at the age of twelve, had taken over as head of the family when his father was killed by a shotgun blast. He scratched out a living from the hard and reluctant west Texas soil, finally giving up the farm during World War II, and moving through a string of uninspiring jobs: blacksmith, dock loader, chicken-butcher; and later, night-watchman.

He did it all with no murmur of complaint, determined to make a living for his family, and fully expecting, with the earnest piety of a backcountry Methodist, greater rewards in the life yet to come. Along the way, as Larry King wrote, "he had the misfortune to sire a hedonist son," and by the time Larry reached the age of fifteen, the two were at each other's throats. They even fought physically on one occasion, and as the younger King remembered it later, "it was savage and ugly—though, as those things go, one hell of a good fight. Only losers emerged, however. After that we spoke in terse mumbles or angry shouts, not to communicate with civility for three years."

It proved to be a long way back, tentative gestures scattered through the years, most often initiated by The Old Man. Slowly, however, a gradual reconciliation emerged, culminating in a trip across Texas just a few weeks before The Old Man died. It was something they had talked about for a while, a pilgrimage to the state capitol in Austin—a distant destination that, in the daily grind of Clyde King's world, he had assumed that he would never see. They set out in the summer of 1970, humming along past the oil fields and desert sand dunes, until finally they came to the hill country of Austin—lush by the dusty standards of home.

One realized as The Old Man grew more and more enthusiastic over roadside growths and dribbling little creeks, just how fenced-in he had been for thirty years; knew, freshly, the depth of his resentments as gas pumps, hamburger outlets, and supermarkets came to prosper within two blocks of his door. The Old Man had personally hammered and nailed his house together, in 1944, positioning it on the town's northmost extremity as if hoping it might sneak off one night to seek more bucolic roots.

On several occasions before their final trip, King had tried to write about his father—encouraged in that delicate ambition by his editor, Willie Morris, at *Harper's*. But the words wouldn't come. Or at least they somehow refused to take on a shape, or to incorporate the subtle shadings of character that this most personal of subjects required. Even after the satisfying journey to Austin, which he hoped might also serve as research, King was still not ready to write. But there were moments that stayed in his mind, mental snapshots that refused to go away, and before long—for reasons that he would later explain—the dam on his writer's block finally broke, and a rush of images poured forth: a four-week binge of forty thousand words that he eventually trimmed back to twelve. There was this, for example, from a thirty-dollar motel room in Austin:

That night he sat on his motel bed recalling the specifics of forgotten cattle trades, remembering the only time he got drunk (at age sixteen) and how the quart of whiskey so poisoned him that he had promised God and his weeping mother that, if permitted to live, he would die before touching another drop. He recited his disappointment in being denied a preacher's credentials by the Methodist hierarchy on the grounds of insufficient education. "They wanted note preachers," he said contemptuously. "Wasn't satisfied with preachers who spoke sermons from the heart and preached the Bible pure. And that's what's gone wrong with the churches."

A few years later, after the article was published to great acclaim in *Harper's*, I ran into King one night in Washington. He was at a Georgetown club called the Cellar Door, and though I had never met him, I told him I had been moved by his story. He seemed pleased.

"You know," he said, and I remember this clearly, "I couldn't write that story until The Old Man died."

In 1974, with the publication of *The Old Man and Lesser Mortals*, a collection of his magazine work, King offered more reflections on the title story. He recounted how, in flying back to Texas for the funeral, he gazed at the clouds outside the plane and seemed to sense, in their shifting shapes, certain mystical intimations about his father. And then came an image that was more concrete. During his final goodbye before an open casket, King noticed his father's weathered hands, folded peacefully on his chest.

They told the story of a countryman's life in the eloquent language of
wrinkles, veins, old scars and new. The Old Man's hands always bore some
fresh scratch or cut as an adornment, the result of his latest tangle with a
scrap of wire, a rusted pipe, a stubborn root; in death they did not disappoint
even in that small and valuable particular. No, it is not given to sons to know
everything of their fathers—mercifully, perhaps—but I have those hands in
my memory to supply evidence of the obligations he met, the sweat he gave,
the honest deeds performed. I like to think you could look at those hands and
read the better part of The Old Man's heart.

Two hours later, when the funeral was done, Willie Morris called
to share his condolences. Larry King thanked him and then blurted
out, "Willie, I can write it now."

In telling that story King offered, I think, an insight into the
writer's obsession—not a particularly attractive quality on the grand
human scale—but most of us writers have it: that final and somehow
inevitable distance from even the most personal of moments that
can make us want to pull back and write. Yes, it is true that we try to
capture and put into words some of those feelings that pour from the
heart; but sadly enough, it is insufficient simply to feel them, to live
the experience as most people do. Whatever the cost, to ourselves or
other people, we are driven instead to write it all down. In seeing that
beautiful demon in King, I recognized, as I reveled in *The Old Man*
and Lesser Mortals, the same incurable malady in myself.

I also remember my feelings of envy that King had Willie Morris
as his editor. For four glorious years, from 1967 until a crash-and-burn
ending in 1971, Morris served as editor-in-chief of *Harper's*—an ac-
complishment made more remarkable by the fact that when it began,
Morris was only thirty-two. At a dinner party during that first year,
he was introduced to U.S. Senator Robert Kennedy.

"You're the editor of *Harper's*?" Kennedy asked, with what seemed to be a kind of wry admiration. "And they tell me you're thirty-two? You must be smart."

Very few people ever doubted that fact. Morris was a Mississippian by birth, coming of age in the town of Yazoo City, which lies at the edge of a string of hills that abruptly give way to the Mississippi Delta. "On a quiet day after a spring rain this stretch of earth seems prehistoric," Morris wrote in *North Toward Home*, a memoir published as he took over *Harper's*, "damp, cool, inaccessible, the moss hanging from the giant old trees—and if you ignore the occasional diesel, churning up one of these hills on its way to Greenwood or Clarksdale or Memphis, you may feel you are in one of those sudden magic places of America, known mainly to the local people and merely taken for granted, never written about, not even on any of the tourist maps."

At the age of seventeen, Morris left Yazoo City for the University of Texas, where he served as editor of the student newspaper and angered some of the powers in Austin with his editorials against segregation and censorship. He graduated in 1956 and headed to England on a Rhodes Scholarship, where, on a side trip to Paris, he met his fellow Mississippian Richard Wright. In recounting that meeting in *North Toward Home*, Morris says he asked Wright, as they talked one night in a little Arab bar, "Will you ever come back to America?"

"No," said Wright. "I want my children to grow up as human beings."

It should be noted, just for the record, that Morris was not above stretching the truth. He once declared on the *David Frost Show* that he had met William Faulkner, which he had not. But by the time he made it to *Harper's*, truthful name-dropping was not a problem for him. During his brief, meteoric tenure, Morris persuaded some of the finest writers in the country, most of whom would become his friends, to contribute their finest work to *Harper's*. From William

Styron came a 45,000-word excerpt of *The Confessions of Nat Turner.* From Norman Mailer, 90,000 words—the longest magazine article ever published—about an anti-war march on the Pentagon, which, as a book, *The Armies of the Night*, won a Pulitzer Prize and a National Book Award.

Morris also had his own stable of regulars—Larry L. King, Marshall Frady, David Halberstam, Peter Schrag—all of whom were deft practitioners of transforming journalism into art. Not that they had a corner on the market. Tom Wolfe, if anything, has received more notice over the years as the leading apostle of "the new journalism." Born in Richmond, Virginia, in 1931, Wolfe earned a Ph.D. in American Studies in 1957, and hated graduate school with such an unhealthy passion that he fled to the low-rent world of newspapers—ultimately to the *New York Herald Tribune*, where he found a newsroom so unkempt ("a promiscuous heap of junk") that he thought it must be journalistic heaven.

One of his *Herald Tribune* colleagues was columnist Jimmy Breslin, "a good-looking Irishman," as Wolfe described him, "with a lot of black hair and a wrestler's gut . . . a bowling ball fueled with liquid oxygen." Once in 1965, Breslin made a trip to Alabama, traveling from Montgomery through the rolling countryside of Lowndes County, a haunted landscape of low-lying swamps and Black Belt prairie, resembling, oddly, something in South Dakota or Kansas. Breslin's destination was the village of Hayneville where the accused killers of Viola Liuzzo—a civil rights worker shot to death on a lonely stretch of Lowndes County highway—were about to go on trial.

In some ways, Breslin covered the story like any other reporter, churning out his copy for a daily deadline, but throwing in unexpected details—a mule grazing in a field near the courthouse, a deputy sheriff spitting out the window, a defense attorney with a pair of pistols in his briefcase and a Klan insignia on his lapel. It seemed to Wolfe, particularly in the early 1960s, that Breslin was engaged in a new enterprise, producing what were, in effect, short stories "complete with symbolism" and novelistic detail, but all on deadline and all within the bounds of the literal truth.

Soon there were other practitioners of the craft, working in forms even more sophisticated—Gay Talese profiling Joe Louis in the pages of *Esquire*, presenting a portrait, not of a sports hero in his prime but of an aging champion trying to find some meaning in his life. Even more ambitiously in 1966, there was Truman Capote's *In Cold Blood*, the book-length account of a quadruple homicide in Kansas—a random crime by a pair of drifters, neither with the gumption to do it alone, reconstructed by Capote in all its nihilistic detail.

Last but not least in Wolfe's estimation was the splendid work he was doing himself, most of it for the *Herald Tribune* and *Esquire*. Some of the pieces he turned into books, culminating in 1979 with *The Right Stuff*, his iconic story of America's astronauts. Wolfe's article of faith, his cornerstone understanding of his craft, was that all the devices available to the novelist—extended dialogue, point of view, the careful development of character and plot—were available to the nonfiction writer as well. The key was to push reporting to a whole new level, gathering information that more conventional journalists might regard as out of reach.

"Your main problem as a reporter," Wolfe wrote, "is, simply, managing to stay with whomever you are writing about long enough for the scenes to take place before your own eyes."

The kinds of scenes Wolfe had in mind were like the following from "Mau-Mauing the Flak Catchers," an essay written in 1970 about an anti-poverty office in San Francisco, where a curious ritual played out periodically. Ghetto radicals of various persuasions would descend on the office and badger some poor and hapless bureaucrat, who in turn would fidget and squirm but offer them almost nothing in return.

"Well," says the Flak Catcher, "I can't promise you jobs if the jobs are not available yet"—and then he looks up as if for the first time he is really focusing on the thirty-five ghetto hot dogs he is now facing, by way of sizing up the threat, now that the shit has started. The blacks and the Chicanos he has no doubt seen before, or people just like them, but then he takes in the Filipinos. There are about eight of them, and they are all wearing Day-Glo yellow and hot-green sweaters and lemon-colored pants and Italian-style socks. But it's the headgear that does the trick. They've all got on Rap Brown shades and Russian Cossack hats made of frosted-gray Dynel. They look bad. Then the man takes in the Samoans and they look worse. There's about ten of them, but they fill up half the room. They've got on Island shirts with designs in streaks and blooms of red, only it's a really raw shade of red, like that red they paint the floor with in the tool and dye works. They're glaring at him out of those big dark wide brown faces. The monsters have tight curly hair, but it grows in long strangs, and they comb it back flat, in long curly strangs, with a Duke pomade job. They've got huge feet, and they're wearing sandals. The straps on the sandals look like they were made from the reins on the Budweiser draft horses . . .

I loved Wolfe's writing the first time I read it. How could you not? It was all so colorful and entertaining, so irreverent and bold, and his own regard for what he was doing was not the least bit modest: "dethroning the novel . . ." he wrote in 1973, "starting the first new direction in American literature in half a century." Not that he gave himself all the credit. There were twenty or so others he also admired, swashbuckling "new journalists" like Hunter S. Thompson, who wrote about those bizarre, hidden corners of American life—the Hell's Angels, for example—that lent themselves to a style as outrageous as Wolfe's. I remember trying it myself one time, writing an article under the influence of Wolfe, and among the greatest of its aesthetic disasters was that it actually got published.

There was something about Wolfe's brand of brilliance—a relationship with many of his subjects that seemed to resemble a heat-seeking missile—and for many of us it simply didn't work. Over time, I came to believe that the missing ingredient, despite all the flash and dazzle and style, was heart: intimations of empathy, or even of respect, for many of the people he chose to write about. In *Harper's*, however, heart was a quality I found in abundance—in the work of Willie Morris and his quite remarkable stable of writers.

II

I don't remember when I first read David Halberstam. It may have been a *Harper's* article, "The Very Expensive Education of McGeorge Bundy," which later grew into *The Best and the Brightest*, perhaps the most admired of Halberstam's books.

Before he began his career as a journalist, Halberstam was a Harvard man, which connotes his level of intellect but not necessarily his view of the world. Upon graduation he headed south to Mississippi and took a job with a small-town paper, the West Point *Daily Times Leader*, where he knew he could cover a little of everything. He also knew in 1955 that Mississippi would put him squarely in the middle of the gathering storm over civil rights, and he wanted to be where history was being made.

Halberstam always seemed to operate on that margin between journalism and history, moving on from Mississippi to cover the Nashville sit-ins for the morning newspaper in that city, before finally landing at the *New York Times*. There, he covered the war in Vietnam, arriving in that ravaged countryside just as America was increasing its role. On June 11, 1963, he witnessed the self-immolation of Thich Quang Duc, a monk protesting the oppression of Buddhists by the government of South Vietnam.

In those early years, Halberstam was one of a handful of reporters who wrote with increasing skepticism about America's Vietnamese allies—and soon about those U.S. generals who kept seeing "light at the end of the tunnel." His work quickly won him a Pulitzer Prize, and then as later, the widespread admiration of his peers.

"Halberstam," wrote Larry L. King, "was . . . a man of utmost integrity whose bullshit detector was infallible . . . He was as intent as a Super Bowl linebacker and just as likely to tackle anybody who intruded on his territory. He may be the most fearless man I ever met."

One of Halberstam's lesser known writings about Vietnam was a brief biography of Ho Chi Minh, an extended essay of 40,000 words published in 1971. I found *Ho*, as the book was known, to be as revealing as any single thing I read about the war. It was rare indeed for a western journalist to attempt, objectively and without polemics, to enter the mind of Ho Chi Minh, the Communist ruler of North Vietnam and maddening adversary of the United States. "Ho Chi Minh," Halberstam wrote, "was one of the extraordinary figures of this era—part Gandhi, part Lenin, all Vietnamese. He was, perhaps more than any single man of the century, the living embodiment to his own people—and to the world—of their revolution."

Born sometime around 1890, Ho had lived through colonial oppression by the French, by the Japanese during World War II, and by the French again in their ill-fated war in the 1950s. Always an enigma, a Communist who quoted the American Declaration of Independence,

Ho was, as Halberstam understood him, a Vietnamese nationalist all the way to the core.

"He was the gentle Vietnamese," Halberstam wrote, "humble, soft-spoken, mocking his own position, always seen in the simplest garb, his dress making him barely distinguishable from the poorest peasant—a style that Westerners for many years mocked, laughing at the lack of trappings of power, of uniform, of style, until one day they woke up and realized that this very simplicity, . . . this capacity to walk simply among his own people was basic to his success."

Despite his Communist ideology, which so troubled the makers of American foreign policy, Ho became for the Vietnamese people a powerful symbol of their urge to be free. He had inspired in them a willingness to fight for as long as it took, and thus the American war effort—a high-minded attempt, when it began, to stop the spread of Asian communism—was doomed. The only question was how much pain we were willing to inflict—upon the Vietnamese and upon ourselves. That was the message of Halberstam's reporting, controversial at the time (and perhaps even today), but to me the highest calling of the craft: speaking the truth, even to people who don't want to hear it.

I think I sensed about Halberstam then what Willie Morris would write of him later: "I had never met a man, and never would, with such a blend of belligerence and sweetness, nor one who so loved the possibilities of America."

Of all of Halberstam's work in those days, there was one book in particular that became for me a temporary obsession. I was in my early twenties then, contemplating a career in journalism, but drawn also to the great political struggles of the times. More specifically, I was drawn to U.S. Senator Robert Kennedy, who, in 1968, was making a star-crossed run for the presidency.

Halberstam set out to cover that run, first in a lengthy profile for

Harper's, and then in a book with the poignant title, *The Unfinished Odyssey of Robert Kennedy*. I thought it was political reporting at its best, reminding me a little, in 1968, of Theodore White's *The Making of the President, 1960*, which I had read in high school. But Halberstam's work was even stronger, not quite detached, but guided by a kind of hardheaded respect as he picked up Kennedy's story in 1967. In September, a young peace activist named Allard Lowenstein, a friend and informal adviser to Kennedy, urged him strongly to run for president—not in 1972, when most political pundits agreed that Kennedy would be the odds-on favorite, but immediately, in 1968, when the country seemed to be coming apart: mired in the war in Vietnam, defined by issues of poverty and race, divided by riots in the inner cities every summer, and led by a president, Lyndon B. Johnson, who seemed to embody everything that was wrong.

That was Lowenstein's view, and to some extent it was Kennedy's too, but in the fall of 1967 Kennedy played Hamlet, unable to decide if he would make the race. To challenge a sitting president in his own party—a powerful, vindictive incumbent—and to come up short would be, for Kennedy, the self-destruction of his political future. So Lowenstein moved on, eventually persuading Eugene McCarthy, a cool, cerebral, anti-war senator from Minnesota, to become the candidate of the "Dump Johnson" movement.

Then in 1968 all hell broke loose. On January 31, Communist forces attacked more than a hundred cities in South Vietnam, shattering the illusion that the war was going well, and providing a sudden, unexpected surge for McCarthy. Kennedy began to rethink his decision not to run, but still he waited. On March 12, McCarthy won a surprising 42 percent of the vote in the New Hampshire primary, demonstrating the vulnerability of President Johnson, and four days later Kennedy entered the race.

By any standard the decision was graceless and poorly timed. "The Kennedys," conceded historian Arthur Schlesinger, "always do these things badly." But Kennedy, as Halberstam noted, suddenly seemed like a man set free. He campaigned with passion in the Indiana primary where he somehow managed to win the support of inner-city blacks and blue-collar whites, two groups who viewed each other with suspicion. And then came the shattering word in April that Martin Luther King Jr. had been murdered in Memphis. Kennedy heard the news on a plane to Indianapolis where he was scheduled to appear at a campaign rally in the inner city. All across the country ghettos were burning, with mobs and looting and scattered sniper fire, but Kennedy insisted on keeping his appointment.

Standing alone on a flatbed truck, hunched against the cold, he told the crowd what had happened to King, and when the people cried out in disbelief he told them he understood how they felt:

Martin Luther King dedicated his life to love and to justice for his fellow human beings, and he died because of that effort. In this difficult day, in this difficult time for the United States, it is perhaps well to ask what kind of a nation we are and what direction we want to move in. For those of you who are black—considering the evidence there evidently is that they were white people who were responsible—you can be filled with bitterness, with hatred and a desire for revenge. We can move in that direction as a country in great polarization—black people amongst black, white people amongst white, filled with hatred toward one another.

Or we can make an effort, as Martin Luther King did, to understand and to comprehend and to replace that racial violence, that stain of bloodshed that has spread across our land, with an effort to understand with compassion and love . . . My favorite poet was Aeschylus. He wrote: "In our sleep, pain which cannot forget falls drop by drop upon the heart until in our own despair, against our will, comes wisdom through the awful grace of God."

Kennedy had reason to understand that despair, for until November of 1963 he had lived his life on behalf of his brother. He had been John Kennedy's campaign manager, his attorney general and top adviser in the White House. Then came Dallas, and as Bobby climbed slowly from the depths of his grief, searching for some new meaning in his life, he identified powerfully with people who hurt—children going hungry in the Mississippi Delta, migrant workers eking out a living in California, American Indians on desolate reservations where there were simply no jobs at all.

As it happened, I had met Robert Kennedy some two weeks before the death of Dr. King. He had come to Nashville on a campaign stop, and I was his student host that night, introducing him to a crowd of 11,000 people. On the drive from the airport to Vanderbilt University, I shared the backseat with Kennedy and John Glenn, the astronaut turned Ohio politician, while in the front seat were three local Democrats. These were prominent men in the party, eager to tell Kennedy what he should and shouldn't say. This is a campus audience, they declared, so talk about the war as much as you want. But it's also the South, so go a little easy on poverty and race.

Kennedy listened briefly, then turned to me and asked without warning, "What do you think I should say?"

I hesitated then told him I thought he should talk about the war, but also about poverty and injustice at home. I said it was true that in the South these subjects were hard but that was all the more reason to discuss them.

"Thank you," said Kennedy, with what I thought was the trace of a smile, "that's what I'll do."

A decade after all the ruined hope of that spring and Kennedy's own death at the hands of still another assassin, I met David Halberstam at a party—a Manhattan book-signing for a mutual friend—and after it was over I told him how much I admired his work. Not only *The Best and the Brightest*, I said, but his earlier, lesser-known book about Kennedy. I told him of my own encounter with the candidate and how genuine and unaffected he had seemed—how he reveled, or so I thought, in rejecting the political advice of the pros.

Halberstam listened to the story with interest, or at least with kindness, for the role of mentor came to him easily. "I think you should write it," he said. When I finally did, I tried to make it good. The bar, after all, had been set very high.

III

I also met Willie Morris one time. On an evening in 1974, he was with Larry L. King at the Cellar Door, the listening room in Washington, D.C., where the finest folk singers in the country often played. The featured act that night was Mickey Newbury, one of King's fellow Texans, best known for composing "An American Trilogy," a medley of "Dixie," "All My Trials," and "The Battle Hymn of the Republic," recorded most movingly by Elvis Presley. I was working on a book on folk and country music, and had come to the club to hear Newbury. When I introduced myself before the show, Newbury was characteristically gracious, and invited me and my handful of friends to "come on over and sit with us."

"Us" turned out to be Willie Morris and King. I couldn't have been more excited, for these were, after all, my journalistic heroes, but as soon as Newbury made the introductions I realized the evening might be an adventure. This was an especially bad time for Morris, not long after he resigned at *Harper's* in a bitter dispute with the magazine's owners—money men concerned with the bottom line, which at *Harper's* had never been very good. But the writing, of course, under Morris was splendid, and when he finally left, unable to take the meddling anymore, most of the finest writers went with him.

Later, all of them would recover—Morris, King, Halberstam and the others—turning out brilliant books for the rest of their careers. But the ending at *Harper's* was painful and hard, and for Morris especially, always a connoisseur of good whiskey, it set off a period of drunken despair. This particular night came at the very depth of his despond. He was as wasted as any man I've ever seen, his eyelids drooping, his head slumping heavily toward his chest.

"God damn!" he slurred as we were introduced. It was a phrase he would utter for the rest of the evening, every time, in fact, Mickey Newbury would finish a song. Deeply moved by the music, Morris would turn and put his hand on my knee, repeating his mantra as if it were something only he and I understood: "God damn!" When the concert ended—and it was stunning in its beauty—he managed to lurch to his feet and drape an arm around Newbury's shoulder. "Mickey" he declared, and here it came again: "God damn, Mickey, you're a poet!"

In the greater scheme of things, I was never quite sure what the evening meant, or why I could never get it out of my mind. Certainly, it was a reminder of the human condition, how complicated and fragile it can be, and I suppose it was ballast for the hero worship that I might otherwise have fallen into. But maybe it was more, perhaps a lesson about artists and art and the alchemy that fascinated Albert Murray—truth and beauty from an anguished heart.

The fiction writers had always understood it, and now Willie Morris and his band of brothers, whatever their foibles and feet of clay, had found the same magic in journalism, in their own understanding of the literal truth.

· 5 ·
_____

Darkness

I

IN THE SPRING of 1985 I did an interview with one of my journalistic heroes. Jacobo Timerman was the editor of *La Opinion*, an opposition newspaper in Buenos Aires, which had set out bravely in the 1970s to expose the excesses of the Argentine government. Timerman was not a native of the country. He spent his first five years in the little Ukrainian village of Bar, where a community of Jews lived with the ancient memory of genocide. In 1648, the Cossack chieftain Chmielnitski descended on the town and murdered all the Jews he could find. Writing in 1981, Timerman offered this history of Bar, and the way it shaped his view of the world:

The community . . . assumed that something as brutal as the existence of Cossack murderers could only be God's final test before the coming of the Messiah. So staunch was their conviction that in 1717 they constructed their Great Synagogue, receiving permission beforehand from the bishop. I attended that synagogue with my father, his six brothers, and all my cousins, and bear within me still a vague longing for those tall, bearded, unsmiling men.

In 1941, when the Nazis entered Bar, they set that synagogue on fire, burning many Jews to death. All the other Jews of Bar plus others from the environs, including the Timermans . . . were killed by the Nazis in October of 1942. Some twelve thousand within a couple of days. My father, happily, had left Bar for Argentina in 1928.

Growing up in South America, Timerman became a passionate Zionist, by which he meant not only the creation of a Jewish homeland—a necessity in the wake of Hitler's Holocaust—but also a love of generosity and justice, a worldwide struggle for human freedom. "I became destined for that world I would never abandon . . ." he wrote, "that world, unique in its beauty and martyrdom, that mythology of pain and memory, that cosmic vision imbued with nostalgia . . ."

Such irrepressible idealism pushed Timerman toward a career in writing, and for more than thirty years he plied his trade as a journalist—a political journalist in the broadest sense, for as time went by he became more and more absorbed in the struggle for human rights. By the 1970s, it was a dangerous preoccupation, for Argentina had splintered into violence, with right-wing death squads and leftist guerillas and a government that, in its struggle against terrorism, became terrorist itself. Depending on whose estimate you accept, somewhere between twelve thousand and thirty thousand Argentines simply disappeared, spirited away in the night, or sometimes in broad daylight, by sinister Ford Falcons with no license plates.

As an editor, Timerman sought to expose the terrorists in his country—right-wing, left-wing, he didn't really care; nor did he spare the Argentine military. In 1977, on an April morning at dawn, twenty men burst into his apartment and led him away in handcuffs. They threw him down on the floor of a car, a blanket tossed roughly over his head, and when they stopped, one of the men put a revolver to his temple. "I'm going to count to ten," he said. "Say goodbye, Jacobo dear." When the counting stopped the man simply laughed, but soon the torture began in earnest—beatings, electrical shocks, solitary confinement for weeks at a time, and still no charges against him were filed. But the most disconcerting thing, curiously enough, he thought looking back, was that his captors seemed to hate him for being a Jew. In *Prisoner Without a Name, Cell Without a Number*, the first of two anguished books he wrote in the 1980s, Timerman offers this account of his torture:

> *I keep bouncing in the chair and moaning as the electric shocks penetrate my clothes. During one of these tremors, I fall to the ground, dragging the chair. They get angry, like children whose game has been interrupted, and again start insulting me. The hysterical voice rises above the others: "Jew . . . Jew . . ."*

Timerman was eventually freed by his captors, in part because of the human rights intervention of U.S. President Jimmy Carter. In an interview in 1985, Timerman told me of his first meeting with Carter, a few years after his release: "We were looking at each other. We are almost the same height, and our faces were at the same level. I said to him, 'How do you feel looking at my face, knowing that you saved my life?'"

For Timerman it was a moment out of time, an instant when history doubled back on itself, and hope and justice became something real. But he had no illusions that it would last. "It was the first time, and I fear the last," he said, "in this violent and criminal century that a major power has defended human rights all over the world."

In the years since, I've thought often about that quote, in part for what it says about Carter, a president who has never quite gotten his due, but also for what it says about the times. What a bleak assessment of the century in which we had lived. But Timerman, of course, was not alone in that view. For many Europeans the very notion of human progress died in the trenches of World War I, for this was when the face of warfare changed, when the *machine* gun—such an ominous juxtaposition of words—became every army's weapon of choice, and in its clinical efficiency, undermined old notions of gallantry and courage.

Patented in 1862 by an American inventor named Richard Gatling, this new kind of gun, by the turn of the century, could fire fifty rounds per second—a feat that the generals found hard to comprehend. As the battle lines were drawn across the face of Europe, the armies on both sides feinted and charged, just as armies had done in the past. This time, however, they were cut to pieces. On April 9, 1917, the British army under Douglas Haig launched an attack on the German lines and lost 160,000 men in a single battle. It was a catastrophic moment in human history, a war in which sixteen million people would die.

It was, however, a mere foreshadowing of World War II, when the death toll would reach sixty million. Nearly twelve million died in the Holocaust, including six million Jews, and thus it should come as no surprise that the great Jewish writers would sketch the horror of the times so clearly. Jacobo Timerman was one of those writers, but there are others more well-known. Elie Wiesel, for example, was an Auschwitz survivor who first told his story in a book called *Night*, one hundred and eight pages of unrelenting horror that begins with an anecdote of denial. In 1942, when Wiesel was a boy in the Romanian town of Sighet, there was a Jew named Moshe whom the villagers regarded as crazy.

"Jews, listen to me," he would cry. "It's all I ask of you. I don't want money or pity. Only listen to me." And then he would tell them what he had seen when the Gestapo carried him away to Poland: "The Jews . . . were made to dig huge graves. And when they had finished their work, the Gestapo began theirs. Without passion, without haste, they slaughtered their prisoners. Each one had to go to the hole and present his neck. Babies were thrown into the air and machine gunners used them as targets."

But the people in the village refused to listen. "And as for Moshe," wrote Wiesel, "he wept."

Soon the people understood that this strange old man was telling the truth. But it was too late. In the spring of 1944, still half believing that nothing so terrible could really be happening, the Jews of Sighet were herded into cattle cars, eighty in every car, crowded there so tightly together that they had to take turns in order to sit down. After three days' travel they came to Auschwitz, where they first saw the flames of the crematoria, first encountered the smell of burning flesh. On the fourth day, Wiesel saw flames leaping from a ditch and a wagonload of babies being burned alive. And then came the hanging, two adults and a child mounted on chairs.

"Where is God? Where is He?" someone behind me asked.

At a sign from the head of the camp, the three chairs tipped over.

Total silence throughout the camp. On the horizon, the sun was setting . . .

Then the march past began. The two adults were no longer alive. Their tongues hung swollen, blue-tinged. But the third rope was still moving; being so light, the child was still alive . . .

For more than half an hour he stayed there, struggling between life and death, dying in slow agony under our eyes. And we had to look him full in the face. He was still alive when I passed in front of him. His tongue was still red, his eyes were not yet glazed.

Behind me I heard the same man asking:

"Where is God now?"

And I heard a voice within me answer him:

"Where is He? Here He is—He is hanging here on these gallows . . ."

Elie Wiesel survived the tortures of Auschwitz and imposed a ten-year silence on himself before he tried to write about what he had seen. Even then, he had trouble finding a publisher, for who would want to read these terrible words? But he knew it was important that the story be told, for how could such atrocities be prevented in the future if the world didn't know?

And in fact the world was beginning to know, for a literature of the Holocaust—of these grisly, almost unfathomable times—was beginning to take shape around the innocent words of a teenaged girl. Anne Frank was thirteen when her Jewish family first went into hiding—her mother, father, older sister, and herself, seeking refuge with two other families in an annex above her father's office. Otto Frank was a businessman in Amsterdam when the Germans overran the Dutch resistance and took control of the city. This was 1940, and there were rumors already of the terrible repressions taking place in

Germany. But in Amsterdam things changed slowly. Frank continued to run his business, respected, even beloved, by his non-Jewish workers, especially his assistant Miep Gies.

Miep and her husband Henk were part of a Dutch underground, seeking ways to resist the German oppressors, for they could see that things were getting worse. First, their Jewish friends were required to register in a special census, and a "J" was stamped on their identity cards; then a new edict required them to wear a yellow Star of David on their clothing. That was often the way it happened: in city after city, as the German army swept across Europe, a slow, insidious imposition of rules, all aimed at setting Jews apart; then suddenly, a torrent of repression, ending in a violent roundup of Jews, and cattle cars rolling through the countryside.

Sometimes, oddly, the roundups took an orderly form—a letter arriving at a particular household, ordering the deportation of a family, or sometimes even one member of the family. On July 5, 1942, such a notice came to the Franks, requiring that Margot, Anne's older sister who was then sixteen, present herself for removal to a Nazi labor camp. Already, the family had been preparing a hiding place, expecting to move in another two weeks. But now, frantically, they were forced to disappear right away.

Anne, by then, had begun keeping a diary, addressing her entries to an imaginary friend named Kitty. This was what she wrote on July 8:

Dear Kitty,

Years seem to have passed between Sunday and now. So much has happened, it is just as if the whole world had turned upside down. But I am still alive, Kitty, and that is the main thing, Daddy says.

Yes, I am still alive, indeed, but don't ask where or how. You wouldn't understand a word, so I will begin by telling you what happened on Sunday afternoon.

At three o'clock . . . someone rang the front doorbell. I was lying lazily reading a book on the veranda in the sunshine, so I didn't hear it. A bit later, Margot appeared at the kitchen door looking very excited. "The S.S. have sent a call-up notice for Daddy," she whispered . . . When we were alone together in our bedroom, Margot told me that the call-up was not for Daddy, but for her. I was more frightened than ever and began to cry. Margot is sixteen; would they really take girls of that age away alone? But thank goodness, she won't go. Mummy said so herself; that must be what Daddy meant when he talked about us going into hiding.

Into hiding—where would we go, in a town or the country, in a house or a cottage, when, how, where . . . ?

Those were the questions I was not allowed to ask . . .

I was about Anne's age when I first read her diary, and like a few million others who also read it, I felt like Kitty—like her lone confidante and best friend. Such was the intimacy of her writing. Re-reading it now, I'm struck once again by the subtlety and wisdom of her words, and more than that, by the sheer and dogged continuity of effort—an unbroken account spanning two years and touching the range of human emotion, resisting a final submission to despair.

She writes of the irritability of confinement as two Jewish families and a member of a third are forced to share cramped quarters above an office, unable to move about except at night for fear of detection by the workers below. As the months go by Anne busies herself with her passion for writing and her studies of history, genealogy, mythology, most often setting an example for the others with her youthful optimism and cheer. All of this comes through in her diary, where she wrote these words at age fifteen:

It's really a wonder that I haven't dropped all my ideals, because they seem so absurd and impossible to carry out. Yet I keep them, because in spite of everything I still believe that people are really good at heart. I simply can't build up my hopes on a foundation consisting of confusion, misery, and death. I see the world gradually being turned into a wilderness, I hear the ever approaching thunder, which will destroy us too. I can feel the sufferings of millions and yet, if I look up into the heavens, I think that it will come right, that this cruelty will end, and that peace and tranquility will return again.

Two weeks later, on August, 4, 1944, the dreaded knock on the door finally came, and the Franks were arrested and taken away to Auschwitz. Otto Frank managed to survive, and though he knew that his wife did not, he had the highest hopes for his daughters. He learned at the liberation of Auschwitz that they had been sent to Bergen-Belsen, a work camp where there were no gassings. There was, however, an epidemic of typhus that claimed both girls just a few weeks before they would have been freed. Anne Frank was fifteen, Margot eighteen.

On the day that the news arrived of their deaths, Miep Gies entered the office of her boss, and handed him a sheaf of papers with an orange-checkered diary on the top. She had found them after the Gestapo raid of August 4, and had put them away unread, waiting for the day that Anne would return. Now she gave them to Mr. Frank. "Here is your daughter's legacy to you," she said.

Frank read the diaries with a mounting sense of amazement: the honesty, the vitality of the voice, even the awkward revelations of tension in the family—all of these were rendered with a grace that touched the father's heart. He began to share the writings with friends, some of whom urged him to have them published, and in 1947 he agreed. A Dutch edition, entitled *Het Achterhuis*, or *The Secret Annexe*, appeared in Amsterdam that year, and in 1952, after sales of more than nine hundred thousand, *Anne Frank: The Diary of a Young Girl* was published in the United States. Now, of course, sales are in the millions.

Eleanor Roosevelt, the former First Lady, spoke for many of those readers when she wrote: "Anne Frank's account of the remarkable changes wrought upon eight people hiding out from the Nazis for two years during the occupation of Holland, living in constant fear and isolation, imprisoned not only by the terrible outward circumstances of war but inwardly by themselves, made me intimately and shockingly aware of war's greatest evil—the degradation of the human spirit. At the same time, Anne's diary makes poignantly clear the ultimate shining nobility of that spirit."

II

Mrs. Roosevelt's assessment, emphasizing nobility of spirit, was in keeping, I think, with the American understanding of the times—a fundamental optimism rooted in the truth. Yes, many terrible things had happened; the Nazi aggressors and their Japanese allies had been unspeakable in their cruelty, but in the end they had been defeated. American might and righteousness prevailed, and that victory produced, understandably, a literature of celebration—celebration, not only of triumph, but also of bravery and shared sacrifice. We had, after all, lived the other side of the story, the side of decency and liberation.

Perhaps the ultimate expression of that point of view was Tom Brokaw's *The Greatest Generation*, his intelligent and finely crafted tribute, published in 1998, to a generation of Americans who had saved the world from the greatest evil in history. Brokaw makes his case with passion, and in the most basic sense I am one of many who agree.

But I have to confess that I'm also drawn to what I would call a literature of dissent—to those American writers who have declared, essentially, "Well, yes, but wait a minute." Joseph Heller, of course, mocks the whole undertaking of war in his absurdist satire, *Catch-22*, and more directly E. B. Sledge writes in his memoir, *With the Old Breed*, of the spirit-killing savagery of combat. But there is more. Kurt Vonnegut also saw major fighting during World War II, and in a letter to his family he described his experience on the Belgian front: "The other American Divisions on our flanks managed to pull out: We were obliged to stay and fight. Bayonets aren't much good against tanks."

Vonnegut was taken prisoner and shipped in a crowded boxcar to Dresden, where he was brutalized by his German captors. But in his letter home, he also wrote of another vivid memory, one he could never put out of his mind:

> *On or about February 14th the Americans came over, followed by the R.A.F. Their combined labors killed 250,000 people in twenty-four hours and destroyed all of Dresden—possibly the world's most beautiful city. But not us. After that we were put to work carrying corpses from Air-Raid shelters; women, children, old men; dead from concussion, fire or suffocation. Civilians cursed us and threw rocks as we carried bodies to huge funeral pyres in the city.*

Twenty-three years later, that memory became a centerpiece for Vonnegut's novel, *Slaughterhouse-Five*, which unfolds with a kind of wry detachment, as if the subject were something very different. "So it goes" becomes Vonnegut's refrain throughout the book, his punctuation for every revelation of tragedy: "She was dead now, had been killed while entertaining troops in the Crimea. So it goes." Or: "His mother was incinerated in the Dresden fire storm. So it goes."

Despite the armor of irony that became his shell, this was not an easy book for Vonnegut to write. "I would hate to tell you," he admits, "what this lousy little book cost me in money and anxiety and time." It was as if the horror of the story were too great, too stark and inexplicable for any person who had actually lived through it, to permit much literary rumination. So Vonnegut wraps the realities of war in a more lighthearted story of science fiction. The central character is Billy Pilgrim, a reluctant soldier and hapless optometrist after the war, who becomes unstuck in time and travels freely from one event in his life to the next. Eventually, he is kidnapped by aliens and taken away to the planet, Tralfamadore, where he is held in captivity with a beautiful actress, Montana Wildhack. The two of them mate, with decreasing self-consciousness, for the fascinated Tralfamadorians, whom Vonnegut describes this way:

> *. . . They were two feet high, and green, and shaped like plumber's friends. Their suction cups were on the ground, and their shafts, which were extremely flexible, usually pointed to the sky. At the top of each shaft was a little hand with a green eye in its palm. The creatures were friendly, and they could see in four dimensions. They pitied Earthlings for being able to see only three.*

Thus does Vonnegut manage to achieve the necessary measure of irony and detachment to tell the story he really wants to tell—how, as a prisoner of war, he rode out the bombing of Dresden in the meat locker of an abandoned slaughterhouse, emerging when it was finally over, to a scene of unbelievable devastation.

> *A guard would go to the head of the stairs every so often to see what it was like outside, then he would come down and whisper to the other guards. There was a fire-storm out there. Dresden was one big flame. The one flame ate everything organic, everything that would burn.*
> *It wasn't safe to come out of the shelter until noon the next day. When the Americans and their guards did come out, the sky was black with smoke. The sun was an angry little pinhead. Dresden was like the moon now, nothing but*

minerals. The stones were hot. Everybody else in the neighborhood was dead.
  So it goes . . .

As readers we are left to make of this what we will—not just the novel, but the truth it reveals. Was it rational, was it just, for Allied bombers to attack this city, one that was largely undefended, and inflict such massive civilian casualties? Estimates of the death toll vary, and Vonnegut's are almost certainly high. But at the time of the attack, February 13–15, 1945, Dresden was a city full of refugees, many of them recent arrivals, fleeing the advance of the Russian Army. Nobody knows how many people were in Dresden at the time, and the bodies in the end were impossible to count. The firestorm left them melted and charred, but the lowest estimate of the dead was twenty-five thousand.

Nor was Dresden the only target of saturation bombing, where civilian casualties were part of the design. In Hamburg the death toll was at least fifty thousand, and then came Hiroshima and Nagasaki where the policy achieved new levels of efficiency and scale. In Hiroshima, the survivors remember August 6, 1945, as a quiet morning with a lone airplane flying overhead, and then a blinding flash of light. "It is an atomic bomb," President Truman told the American people. "It is a harnessing of the basic power of the universe. The force from which the sun draws its power has been loosed against those who brought war to the Far East."

For many Americans, the first full account of the devastation came on August 31, 1946, in a *New Yorker* article written by John Hersey. The article—thirty-one thousand words—filled the magazine's entire issue, and within a few hours every copy had been sold. Earlier, in September of 1945, another reporter named George Weller had filed a detailed report from Nagasaki, just after the second atomic bomb was dropped, but it was censored by the U.S. military. Hersey's was not, and it is regarded by many as perhaps the finest piece of journalism of the twentieth century.

Published later as a book, entitled simply, *Hiroshima*, the article offered this description of the scene at Hiroshima's Red Cross Hospital:

Wounded people supported maimed people; disfigured families leaned together. Many people were vomiting . . . In a city of two hundred and forty-five thousand, nearly a hundred thousand people had been killed or doomed at one blow; a hundred thousand more were hurt. At least ten thousand of the wounded made their way to the best hospital in town, which was altogether unequal to such a trampling, since it had only six hundred beds, and they had all been occupied.

And this from another part of the city, based on an interview with a priest:

The hurt ones were quiet; no one wept, much less screamed in pain; no one complained; none of the many who died did so noisily; not even the children cried; very few people even spoke. And when Father Kleinsorge gave water to some whose faces had been almost blotted out by flash burns, they took their share and then raised themselves a little and bowed to him, in thanks.

U.S. officials, military and civilian, defended the bombings on the grounds of military necessity. Without them, so the argument goes, many more people—certainly many more *Americans*—might have died in the final, bloody conquest of Japan. But regardless of the strategic realities, when reading both Vonnegut and John Hersey, I found it hard to disagree with the *Saturday Review*. Reviewing *Hiroshima*, the magazine declared:

"Everyone able to read should read it."

III

How, in the end, do we understand our own morality as a nation? Is it enough to say that in World War II the Germans and the Japanese were worse? One of the writers who has reflected most eloquently on those kinds of questions is, once again, Jacobo Timerman, the great Jewish author from Argentina. In 1983, he too wrote a lengthy article for the *New Yorker*, one that also became a book, and stirred, like Hersey's, a deluge of commentary at the time.

Following his imprisonment in Argentina, Timerman had been deported to Israel, the mythic sanctuary of his Zionist dreams. He found so much that was beautiful there, so much history, so much to love. His son had been living on a kibbutz, or farming collective, coaxing crops from what had once been a desert. It was a tradition deeply rooted in Israeli history, when Jews at the turn of the twentieth century began to repatriate Palestine—a journey of escape from the persecutions of Europe.

Timerman, of course, recognized the necessity of such a journey, and he regarded the modern state of Israel, whatever its flaws, as a beacon of hope to Jews everywhere—and perhaps to other peoples as well, for there was an idealism about its founding, a commitment not only to self-defense, to the prevention of atrocities like those under Hitler, but also to justice. Israelis fought wars when they were attacked, but only then, for they were a people who wanted only peace. They understood the horrors of war too well.

And yet when Timerman arrived in Israel, he could feel a shift in the political climate, and perhaps in the moral climate as well—all of which played out in an invasion of Lebanon. In 1982, Israeli General Ariel Sharon orchestrated a massive bombardment, and from Timerman's perspective it was fundamentally different from anything his adopted country had ever done. In his impassioned book, *The Longest War*, which grew out of his article for the *New Yorker*, he offered this assessment of the war:

Many things were occurring for the first time. For the first time Israel had attacked a neighboring country without being attacked; for the first time it had mounted a screen of provocation to justify a war. For the first time Israel brought destruction to entire cities: Tyre, Sidon, Damur, Beirut.

And also this:

Every Jew carries within him some old or recent scar from an inflicted humiliation. Heroism is a daily need, and in those first days it came in bundles. But afterward one had to decide whether those burning ruins of Lebanese cities had anything to do with heroism, or whether they were pictures of another war to demonstrate what Jews would be incapable of doing.

A man walks among those ruins, carrying in his arms a child of ten. A group of men, women, and children with their arms raised are under guard, and the expression on their faces, what their eyes say, is easily understood by almost any Jew. Yet we are forbidden to equate today's victims with yesterday's, for if this were permitted, the almost unavoidable conclusion would be that yesterday's crimes are today's.

As I read Jacobo Timerman's words, I thought of another book on Israeli history, a book called *The Prophets*, written by Rabbi Abraham Heschel. Heschel was a remarkable man. In 1965, he marched from Selma to Montgomery with Dr. Martin Luther King Jr., and with his air of solemnity and long, flowing beard, he reminded some of his fellow marchers of God. In his book on the ancient Hebrew prophets—men like Micah, Isaiah, Jeremiah—Heschel offered this summary of their calling: "The prophet is a lonely man. His standards are too high, his stature too great, and his concern too intense for other men to share."

In particular, the prophets expected better things of the Jews, God's chosen people, and deep in his heart Jacobo Timerman shared that perspective. He did it, in fact, without any trace or glimmer of apology. He did not equate the scale of devastation caused by Israel with the massive atrocities committed by Hitler. But even the faintest hint of similarity was more than he could bear, and he believed the similarities were there: a newfound power, perhaps a burgeoning greed, all of it shielded and artfully disguised by memories of suffering in the past.

There were many in Israel who regarded Timerman as an ingrate, criticizing the country that had granted him asylum. Others saw him as remarkably brave, while Timerman, I think, merely saw himself as a writer, trying somehow to issue a warning against the startling human capacity not to learn. At the least, he helped to trigger a debate, which in one form or another, is still going on in Israel today.

IV

But what of this country?

Ever since Sherman's March to the Sea—and certainly in World War II and Vietnam—civilian suffering has been a cornerstone of military strategy, part of America's way of making war. Many of us are unhappy with those, particularly our writers, who are so ill-mannered as to point this out, for it puts a chink in our armor of innocence. This is certainly true in the twenty-first century, when, after the hideous attacks of 9-11, our national state of fright was so intense that we attacked a country that had not attacked us—again with massive civilian casualties—and resorted to torture as an instrument of policy. In 2009, when a new administration came into power, there was a brief discussion of holding those accountable who had thus betrayed our national ideals. But the new administration proved to be timid, and when a leader in the opposition party promised "World War III" (presumably speaking only in metaphor) if any such serious attempt were made, all discussion of accountability ceased.

Many Americans would prefer to leave it that way, rather than explore our national contradictions, reflected in the people we have chosen to lead us. But there are always writers who won't let it rest. In addition to the columnists at magazines like the *Nation*, I found myself reading, during the debate over torture, a writer of great eloquence who had recently died. Marshall Frady had been a Willie Morris protégé at *Harper's*, and in that capacity, had written about the collective character of the country. In 1979, during an unaccustomed interlude of peace, he wrote of "the American Innocence itself—that plain, cheerful, rigorous, ferociously wholesome earnestness which, to some, as one Egyptian editor put it during the days of Vietnam, 'has made you nice Americans the most dangerous people on the face of the earth.'"

The Egyptian editor was wrong about that. We are not the most dangerous people on earth, not in a world that once included Hitler and is still clearly capable of genocide. But perhaps we do, as our writers point out, possess some terrible capacity for violence (often juxtaposed with bravery and sacrifice) that we see so clearly in other parts of the world. We *are* the only nation—at least so far—to actually make use of an atom bomb, and we did it twice, and as the vivid account of John Hersey makes clear, this is not a distinction to be proud of.

· 6 ·

Just Telling a Story

All Creatures Great and Small—James Herriot

Walking Across Egypt—Clyde Edgerton

Clover—Dori Sanders

ALSO, FERROL SAMS, JAMES DICKEY, ROBERT INMAN,
LOUIS RUBIN, ELLEN GLASGOW, KATE CHOPIN,
LEE SMITH, ALICE WALKER

I

THE MEMOIR OF an English veterinarian. Somehow, it didn't sound like a book that I would want to read. But the reviews and the testimonials of friends finally began to wear down my resistance, and James Herriot did not disappoint. From the very first page of *All Creatures Great and Small* I was swept along by the story-telling charm of a gifted writer from an unexpected place. This was 1973, still a troubled time in America with the continued rumblings of racial unrest and a war still raging in Vietnam, and the first intimations of a national scandal that would bring down a president.

As I read Herriot's wry and warm-hearted stories, delivered against this backdrop of gloom, I discovered a most welcome reprieve. This, however, was more than escape. Herriot was not only a fine storyteller, but he was also a man who understood human nature. His real name was James Alfred Wight, and in 1939, at the age of twenty-three, he began a veterinary practice in the Yorkshire Dales, an often cold and windswept land, where a sturdy band of farmers raised their cattle and horses and sheep. For more than twenty years, Herriot simply told his stories by the fire, but he also nursed a desire to write, to capture the humor and wisdom of his neighbors as they coaxed a hard-earned living from the land. He became convinced, as he rumbled along the rutted back roads, that the farther from civilization he traveled, the more fascinating the people seemed to be.

At the bottom of the valley, where it widened into a plain, the farmers were like farmers everywhere, but the people grew more interesting as the land heightened, and in the scattered hamlets and isolated farms near the bleak tops I found their characteristics most marked; their simplicity and dignity, their rugged independence and their hospitality."

Sometimes their stories were touching and sad, as when Herriot told of a visit to a farm where an old man lived alone with his dog, his wife having died the previous year. "He's my only friend now," the old man said. "I hope you'll soon be able to put him right." But Herriot discovered an inoperable tumor, and suggested that the dog—a fourteen-year-old Labrador retriever—be put to sleep. The patient, he explained, was already in pain and it would only get worse.

The old man was silent, then he said, 'Just a minute,' and slowly and painfully knelt down by the side of the dog. He did not speak, but ran his hand again and again over the grey old muzzle and the ears, while the tail thump, thump, thumped on the floor.

He knelt there a long time while I stood in the cheerless room, my eyes taking in the faded pictures on the walls, the frayed, grimy curtains, the broken-springed armchair . . .

Herriot, of course, is not the only writer to tell such stories. Fred Gipson did it earlier in *Old Yeller*, and Willie Morris soon followed with *My Dog Skip*. But in Herriot's case, whatever his tender regard for his patients—the four-legged kind—he was moved most deeply by the grace of their owners. He somehow managed, page after page, to keep his sentimentality at bay, sometimes skating, purposefully, perilously, close to the edge. But in the end his stories displayed a deft sense of timing, a *pacing*, which held the attention of a few million readers, including me.

Throughout the course of more than four hundred pages, we came to share in his irrepressible delight, not that the land and the work weren't hard, even backbreaking, nor feelings of loss a constant possibility in a life spent working so closely with animals. But in these mountains, he found a rhythm and an authenticity, and from time to time a certain perversity in human nature that offered a ready supply of entertainment. Once, for example, Herriot was chatting with a colleague named Grier, a crochety old vet who told him the story of an ungrateful client—a former British admiral who once had Grier examine his horse. Grier warned that the animal had a bad heart, and the admiral, having hoped for a different diagnosis, took the horse to another veterinarian who pronounced him sound. Herriot picks up the story from there:

The admiral wrote Grier a letter and told him what he thought of him in fairly ripe quarter-deck language. Having got this out of his system he felt refreshed and went out for a ride during which, in the middle of a full gallop, the horse fell down dead and rolled on the admiral who sustained a compound fracture of the leg and a crushed pelvis.

"Man," said Grier with deep sincerity, "man, I was awfu' glad."

It so happened that not long after reading James Herriot, I set to work on a first book of my own and was delighted in 1976 when it was accepted for publication by St. Martin's Press. This was Herriot's publisher, and my feelings about *All Creatures Great and Small* only grew warmer when I learned the backstory—confided by a bemused editor—of the press's acceptance of my own modest work. It seems there had been an editorial meeting at which my book was judged to be tidy enough, but questions were raised about whether it would sell. I was, after all, a literary nobody.

"Well," my editor was reported to have said, "we've got James Herriot. I suppose we could take a chance on Gaillard."

II

Not long after this happy development I came upon a new storyteller, another man of healing who plied his trade in Fayetteville, Georgia. Ferrol Sams was a good country doctor, whose patients, unlike Herriot's, tended to be of the human variety. Both writers were products of the same generation, Herriot born in 1916, Sams in 1922, and they had a similar storytelling style: each inclined to see the humor in things, perhaps as ballast for a corollary sadness.

Sams's first novel, *Run with the Horsemen*, appeared in 1982 about the time the author turned sixty. I thought as I settled in with the story that it was unlike any Southern novel I had read. It took me a while to figure out the difference, but then it came to me clear as a bell: there was no urgency or anguish about this book, no particular sense of regional suffering. It was a coming-of-age novel morphing out of memoir, set in Georgia during the Depression. There were inevitable references to poverty and race, but it was primarily a book of gentle recollection with an edginess rooted chiefly in humor.

That was not the case for most Southern writing in the twentieth century. Regardless of the ideology of the author, there was pain at the heart of most Southern stories, a sense of a time and a place deeply troubled. That was certainly the case in 1902 when Thomas Dixon wrote *The Leopard's Spots*, and two years later, a follow-up novel called *The Clansman*. Now largely forgotten, Dixon was arguably the first superstar of Southern letters. Not that we would claim him today. A racist to his core, he believed that blacks had caused the Civil War, and, once freed by the tragic defeat of the South, were returning to a natural state of bestiality.

The remarkable thing about Dixon's premise is that most white people in America believed it. Millions of them read his books, and a few years later he wrote a screenplay with the same basic theme, *The Birth of a Nation*, that soon became the most popular movie of the silent-screen era. In 1915, President Woodrow Wilson arranged a special showing at the White House. He pronounced the story—with its exaltation of the Ku Klux Klan—"so terribly true" and famously said it was "like writing history with lightning."

Ideology aside, it was a story of suffering, and so, of course, was *Gone With the Wind*, which appeared in 1938, as Margaret Mitchell supplanted Thomas Dixon as the most popular Southern writer of her time. Her characters also were sifting through the ruins of the Civil War, filled with nostalgia about the Southern past and feelings of urgency about the future. And then in 1949, when Lillian Smith turned the Old South ideology on its head, she, too, in *Killers of the Dream*, set out to explore the anguished Southern soul.

Much of it had to do with race, though there was also the related issue of poverty—a reality explored directly by James Agee in *Let Us Now Praise Famous Men*, and indirectly in much of Southern fiction, from Robert Penn Warren to Flannery O'Connor. Even as late as 1970, it was present, you could argue, in James Dickey's *Deliverance*, a swashbuckling novel of four city slickers who brave the wilds of the north Georgia mountains. The primary reason for *Deliverance*'s popularity—and it became iconic—was Dickey's great gift as a storyteller; that, and the poetic beauty of his prose:

It unrolled slowly, forced to show its colors, curling and snapping back whenever one of us turned loose. The whole land was very tense until we put our four steins on its corners and laid the river out to run for us through the mountains 150 miles north. Lewis' hand took a pencil and marked out a small strong X in a place where some of the green bled away and the paper changed with the high ground, and began to work downstream, northeast to southwest through the printed woods. I watched the hand rather than the location, for it seemed to have power over the terrain, and when it stopped for Lewis' voice to explain something, it was as though all streams everywhere quit running, hanging silently where they were to let the point be made. The pencil turned over and pretended to sketch in with the eraser an area that must have been around fifty miles long, through which the river hooked and cramped.

"When they take another survey and rework this map," Lewis said, "all this in here will be blue . . ."

Dickey didn't develop these skills by accident. A graduate of

Vanderbilt University where he double-majored in English and philosophy (and minored in astronomy), Dickey was also a football star and former fighter pilot. He began publishing poetry in 1960 and in 1965 his collection, *Buckdancer's Choice*, won a National Book Award. "It has a passionate quality," the *New York Times* said of the collection, ". . . a kind of carefully separated madness that makes it one of the remarkable books of the decade."

In *Deliverance*, his debut novel, Dickey constructed a new sense of madness, an animating danger that sprang from depravity—a predatory violence among the poverty-stricken people of southern Appalachia. So wretched and crazed are these mountain dwellers that they are driven to mayhem, murder and rape, and four suburbanites, who have come to see a mountain river before it is dammed, are caught in a desperate struggle to survive. In James Dickey's mind, the South—even on the precipice of major change—could still be a terrifying place.

But in the writing of Ferrol Sams it was not, and similar books soon followed. In 1987, first-time author Robert Inman, a North Carolinian by way of Alabama, published *Home Fires Burning*, a novel set in a small Southern town. It is a home-front story from World War II: an aging generation of leaders—a newspaper editor, a small-town mayor—awaiting, with double-edged anticipation, the return of their sons from the European theater. They sense already, as the war is winding down, that their own time is beginning to pass, and the future will belong to somebody else. There is thus a seriousness at the heart of the story, but it is written with elegant humor and affection; an author clearly at ease with his place.

"Just telling a story," Inman once explained when I asked him about his hopes for the novel.

It struck me then, intuitively at least, that one reason for this change in the literary South—this kinder, gentler era of Southern writing—

was a shift in the psyche of the region itself. It began to take shape in the 1970s; somewhere in there it dawned on us that we had shed the great albatross of our existence: that officially codified racism which seemed in retrospect to be so absurd. Had we really had white and colored signs? Separate drinking fountains? Requirements for seating in the back of the bus? Not only had these tangible symptoms disappeared, but somehow the civil rights movement itself, which seemed at first to have simply slipped away—as one writer put it, "like a piece of driftwood beneath the surface of the water"—in fact for a time had been largely *absorbed*. Its broader assumptions about brotherhood and justice, if not fully realized, had become a part of mainstream thinking, and the benighted South, now all of a sudden, seemed to be leading the way for the nation.

For a time, at least, that was how it felt, and I can remember precisely the moment when all of these things came into focus. It was the summer of 1976, and a white Southern governor named Jimmy Carter had won his party's nomination for president. Nearly six years earlier Carter burst upon the national scene when he declared in his inaugural address in Georgia, "The time for racial discrimination is over." Now here he was at the Democratic National Convention, sharing the stage with Martin Luther King Sr.—two Georgians, one black, one white, reaching out across the divide. There was a feeling almost of old-time revival as King closed his eyes and declared with a passion that had long been his trademark: "Surely the Lord is in this place."

Whatever the religious implications of the moment, the *Southern* implications were immense, becoming more so the following January when Carter became president of the United States. It was clear to all of us by then that the South was no longer the national stepchild, the perpetual embarrassment that the rest of America didn't want to

discuss. Our celebration spread quickly from politics to culture, beginning with music, as great Southern bands from the Allman Brothers
to Lynard Skynard helped make us proud, unequivocally, at last, to
be the sons of Sweet Home Alabama.

III

When these same feelings spread to literature, when fine Southern
writers no longer felt shackled by apology or shame—or even an ap-
propriate display of Southern anguish—one of my favorites among the
new storytellers would soon become a good friend. Clyde Edgerton
was a North Carolinian by birth, a member of the first generation
in his family to move away from the farm. His daddy's family raised
tobacco, his mama's cotton, and when they moved to the little town of
Bethesda, just outside of Durham, they were still not far from extended
family. There were, by actual count, twenty-three aunts and uncles,
grandparents and cousins, most of them living out in the country,
where young Clyde loved to hunt and fish.

He was an only child, close to both parents, and partly because of
those early years he became that rarest of literary creatures, a happy
writer. As a teenager he was a good student with a good sense of humor,
and his adolescent passions included baseball and music. Edgerton was
fairly good at both, and he also read a little on the side. Mark Twain
was one of his favorites, but his love of literature didn't hit full stride
until he went away to the University of North Carolina. There, he
read Ernest Hemingway's *A Farewell to Arms*, and later the stories of
Flannery O'Connor, and decided he wanted to be an English teacher.

It was the kind of decision he would make several times in the
course of his life: very deliberate and rational, reflecting a healthy,
good-humored confidence that he could accomplish whatever he set

out to do. Military service intervened before he began his career as a teacher (he was a fighter pilot in the U.S. Air Force), but when he came home to North Carolina he took a job at his old high school. He quickly discovered that he loved to teach, loved to share with his students his own growing passion for the written word. He had not yet started to write, but then one day, May 14, 1978, he saw the great Mississippian, Eudora Welty, reading one of her stories on public television.

It was a short story called "Why I Live at the P.O.," an edgy account of family dysfunction, published in *A Curtain of Green*, Welty's first book. So enthralled was Edgerton that he made the following entry in his diary:

"Tomorrow, May 15, 1978, I would like to start being a writer."

Seven years later his first novel appeared, and the critical acclaim was instantaneous. *Raney* told the story of a mixed Southern marriage—the rocky union between a girl who grew up Free Will Baptist and a young man who was raised Episcopalian. Among the humorless within the ranks of Southern Christians, the novel brought forth gasps of horror. But in other quarters it was widely regarded as brilliant satire, and it was chosen by the *New York Times* as one of the notable books of 1985.

"This book is too good to keep to yourself," concluded the *Richmond Times Dispatch*. "Read it aloud with someone you love." And the *New Yorker* praised Edgerton for "his tolerant humor and his alertness to the human genius for nonsense."

For me, those qualities were in even greater abundance in *Walking Across Egypt*, Edgerton's second book. It occurred to me within a few pages that this was one of the funniest, most warmhearted stories that I had ever read, and three or four readings later nothing about that impression has changed. Edgerton told me in one conversation that the book took shape around a story from his mother. It seems that one day at the age of eighty, she had taken a seat in her old, familiar chair without realizing that the bottom had been removed, apparently to be reupholstered. She became stuck and thirty minutes passed before the moment of rescue. Edgerton knew when he heard the story that he had to write it.

He invented the character of Mattie Rigsbee, a seventy-eight-year-old small-town widow who wishes she were a grandmother, but her two grown children have not yet obliged. Mattie talks often about "slowing down," by which she means she's starting to grow a bit forgetful, and one of the things she happens to forget is that she—like Edgerton's mother in real life—has removed the bottom of a rocking chair to have it redone. One day after lunch she goes to her den to watch a soap opera on TV and quickly realizes she has made a mistake:

Ah, the commercial—New Blue Cheer—was still on. She had started sitting down when a mental picture flashed into her head: the chair without a bottom. But her leg muscles had already gone lax. She was on the way down. Gravity was doing its job. She continued on past the customary stopping place, her eyes fastened to the New Blue Cheer box on the TV screen, her mind screaming no, wondering what bones she might break, wondering how long she was going to keep going down, down, down.

Mattie discovers she is thoroughly stuck, her bottom barely an inch from the floor, her arms and legs pointed straight up, and there she remains until a dogcatcher arrives at her house:

He walked around to the backyard, looked for a dog. There: a fice on the back steps. He wondered if that was the dog he was supposed to pick up. The back door was open. He looked in through the screen, glanced down at the

dog. Dog's a little tired or something, he thought. He looked back inside.
"Anybody home?"

"Come in. Please come in."

He opened the door and stepped into the den. The room was dark except
for the TV and someone sitting . . . Damn, she didn't have no neck at all.
That was the littlest person he'd ever . . . Wait a minute. What in the world
was . . . ?

It spoke: "I'm stuck in this chair."

If, as Eudora Welty once said, good writing is a matter of learning
to see, learning to hear, and finding a voice, Edgerton clearly has done
all three. But it is his ear, I think, that sets him apart, his ability to *hear*
the way his characters think and talk. What he hears most in *Walking*
Across Egypt is a kind of relentless, counterintuitive logic coming from
the mind of Mattie Rigsbee. She has lately been reading her Bible a
lot, perhaps a bit more seriously than in the past, and she fixates on
a particular verse.

"That scripture," she says, "Jesus talking about visiting prisoners
and all, was 'Inasmuch as ye have done it unto one of the least of these
my brethren ye have done it unto me.'" It is, of course, one of the
most radical pronouncements in the Bible, and when Mattie begins
to take it seriously, people around her reach the only conclusion they
can—the only one that makes any sense in the small-town world in
which they are living: they assume that Mattie has lost her mind.

Specifically, they are worried that she has taken in a juvenile delin-
quent, a teenager named Wesley Benfield, nephew of the dogcatcher
who saved her from the bottomless chair. Wesley has stolen a car and
been sent away to the Young Men's Rehabilitation Center. When
Mattie goes to visit him there, Wesley is at first astonished, and then
concludes that this old woman must be his grandmother.

Everything unfolds from there in scenes that range from slapstick to poignant. In the process Mattie Rigsbee takes her place, certainly for people who have read this book, as one of the unforgettable characters in American fiction. No matter that *Walking Across Egypt* is fundamentally a lighthearted story, at the opposite end of the literary spectrum from Flannery O'Connor and the Southern Gothic writers that Edgerton admired. This is a splendid piece of storytelling, as cheerful as it is well-crafted, and when it appeared in 1987 Clyde Edgerton, at the age of forty-three, modestly, confidently assumed his role as one of the fine new writers in the country.

Actually, he was part of a movement of sorts, one of several emerging authors discovered in the 1980s by a veteran editor named Louis Rubin. Born in 1923 to a Jewish family in South Carolina, Rubin was a journalist turned literary scholar. His interests were vast, the subjects of his own books ranging from baseball to Jewish history to an early biography of Thomas Wolfe. But his greatest contribution, almost certainly, was the way in which he embodied the link between the Southern literary present and past. In addition to writing about Thomas Wolfe, he also explored the work of Ellen Glasgow, a beautiful, aristocratic Virginian who produced a steady stream of novels from 1897 until 1942, ultimately winning the Pulitzer Prize. Glasgow was a woman ahead of her time, writing *The Descendant* in 1897, a novel in which, as one critic put it, "an emancipated heroine seeks passion rather than marriage," a scandalous choice in Victorian Virginia. Glasgow also wrote *The Ancient Law*, a novel set in the textile mills of Virginia, exploring the social ills of that particular form of capitalism; and she arranged for the posthumous publication of *The Woman Within*, her own writer's memoir. In it she acknowledged, among other things, an extended affair with a married man.

In her fearless honesty, she has been compared by some to Kate

Chopin, another brilliant and beautiful Southerner who began her career in the 1890s. Chopin, writing in her adopted state of Louisiana, first raised eyebrows with her short story, "Desiree's Baby," published in *Vogue* in 1893 and then in her collection, *Bayou Folk*, in 1894. The story, on its face a kind of post-Victorian romance, explored the unexpected themes of miscegenation and racial prejudice. And then in 1899 Chopin stirred even greater controversy with her novel, *The Awakening*, a multilayered story of a woman's sexuality: a startling reflection, or so it was said, of the writer's own romantic life. At the very least she was, like Glasgow, an author who pushed her writing to the edge.

Louis Rubin, who studied the South in all of its dimensions, did not want to see such writers forgotten. In 1957 he joined the faculty of Hollins College in Virginia, and there in addition to his work as a scholar, he helped promote the work of two student writers, Lee Smith and Annie Dillard, both of whom went on to greater fame. Dillard won a Pulitzer Prize in 1974 with the publication of her first book, *Pilgrim at Tinker's Creek*. Smith too became a national best seller, almost as well-known for her generosity to other writers as for her string of brilliant novels, *Oral History, Fair and Tender Ladies*, and *The Last Girls*, among many others.

In 1982, after a stint at the University of North Carolina, Rubin and editor Shannon Ravenel, another Hollins graduate, founded Algonquin Books of Chapel Hill, a national trade publisher based in the South. Some in their impressive stable of new authors wrote with the same artistry and darkness that had long been a staple among Southern writers. Kaye Gibbons's first novel, *Ellen Foster*, explored harsh themes of racism and domestic violence, and in Larry Brown's debut, *Dirty Work*, two hideously wounded military veterans—one black, one white—form a friendship as they lie in adjacent hospital beds.

These were powerful, disturbing books, but other Algonquin authors, including Clyde Edgerton and Jill McCorkle, leavened their serious themes with humor. And there was also Dori Sanders, perhaps the most unusual of Louis Rubin's finds.

Sanders was a peach farmer, an African American from a family still living close to the land. In 1915, her father, Marion Sylvester Sanders, a former sharecropper and son of a slave, bought eighty-one acres near the community of Filbert, South Carolina. Mr. Sanders was a man of intensity and will who worked his way through college, became a public school principal, and instilled in his children—especially Dori, the seventh of ten—a lifelong love of reading and books.

Still, she had never thought seriously of writing one herself until the day in the 1980s when she was working at her family's peach stand. She saw two funeral processions passing by, one white, one black, winding slowly through the rural countryside. Caught in the palpable moment of sadness—these two processions so close together—she was deeply moved by the image of a child waving shyly from the back of a car. Sanders felt her imagination roam, mixing the two processions together, and she wondered what would happen if a child of ten in one of these lines—a little black girl, grieving for her father—found herself alone with a widowed stepmother. And what if the stepmother were white?

For weeks and even months after that, Sanders wrote scenes on scraps of paper, tossing them into a paper bag. Eventually, she pulled them out and began to arrange them on the floor, pondering how a story might fit together. Such was Louis Rubin's skill as an editor that he and his partner, Shannon Ravenel, were able to help Sanders "work it like a puzzle." The result was her debut novel, *Clover*, published in 1990 to rave reviews and almost immediate international acclaim.

"Sanders sews these family scenes together like a fine quilt maker," proclaimed the *Washington Post*. And the *Chicago Tribune* declared: "Sanders writes with wit and authority in this unusual gem of a love story."

What she produced, it seemed to me, was essentially the anti-*Color Purple*. Eight years after Alice Walker's masterpiece, which won a Pulitzer Prize with its scenes of domestic violence and rape, here was a novel full of tenderness and hope. *Clover* was set, like *The Color Purple*, in the rural South, a terrain that Sanders understood well. In *Clover* she offers a confident portrayal, nothing glossed over, no pulled punches, her characters complicated and flawed. But her fictional world is not as hopeless, as fundamentally dehumanized, as the lives of Alice Walker's characters. The world Sanders knew was not that way. It was true that growing up in the 1940s she saw the handiwork of the Ku Klux Klan and felt the insensitivity of racial segregation. But she also came from a family of achievers, loved a father who believed in education. Hers was an extended family who found fulfillment on a farm, and there was also this: through her educator-father she was keenly aware of the possibility of kindness.

She heard him speak with reverence about the philanthropy of Julius Rosenwald, the self-made president of Sears, Roebuck and Company. In the early years of the twentieth century, Rosenwald, working closely with Booker T. Washington, helped build fifteen thousand schools for African American children in the South. Dori herself attended one of those schools, and she heard her father speak often of this Jewish man from Illinois (raised, he noted, just up the street from where Abraham Lincoln had lived) who had left such a powerful legacy of progress.

The simple notion that things can get better, that barriers can fall before the force of good will, is the fundamental story line of *Clover*. It is a message wrapped in the storyteller's art, delivered with the irony and charm of a ten-year-old narrator. Human foolishness and frailty are on full display. But our better angels are present as well, those moments of shared humanity and promise that are also a part of the human condition.

It's a realm that writers need not forsake, and Dori Sanders—like James Herriot, and like Clyde Edgerton—understands the literature of that truth.

· 7 ·

Poetry, Prose, and a Sense of Place

FEATURING:

All the King's Men—Robert Penn Warren

At Play in the Fields of the Lord—Peter Matthiessen

Snow Falling on Cedars—David Guterson

ALSO, T. HARRY WILLIAMS, WILL CAMPBELL

I

I DON'T KNOW when I first read *All the King's Men*. I must have been through it a dozen times by now; it is quite simply my favorite book, and there are passages that I can almost quote:

But all at once the laughter was gone. It was as though someone had pulled a shade down in front of her face. I felt as you do when you pass down a dark street and look up to see a lighted window and in the bright room people talking and singing and laughing with the firelight splashing and undulating over them and the sound of the music drifts out to the street while

you watch; and then a hand, you will never know whose hand, pulls down the shade. And there you are outside.
And there I was, outside.

Every encounter with the poetry of that prose has left me marveling at Robert Penn Warren's ability to produce it—his subtle alliterations and internal rhymes, the waltz-like cadence of the paragraphs; not the jazz riffs of Mark Twain or Albert Murray, but something much easier and sweeter than that, like a stream tumbling gently over the rocks. There are many writers I've admired through the years, but only a handful that have left me in awe. Heresy though it may be, even William Faulkner is not one of those. But Warren is, and perhaps because I am not a poet I come at his writings through the mysteries of verse—which was, after all, his own point of entry to the written word.

In 1921, at age sixteen, he entered Vanderbilt University and while he was there he studied with some of the finest poets of his time, including John Crowe Ransom, Allen Tate, and Andrew Lytle. From 1922 to 1925 a group that included professors and students gathered regularly to talk about poetry. They called themselves the Fugitives, and after a time they began to publish a journal by that name. It never had more than two hundred subscribers, but this dogged little group produced some important poetry for a while and attracted the attention of some of the most prominent poets in the world, including T. S. Eliot. As an undergraduate, Robert Penn Warren was one of the prodigies, and in later years he would go on to win a Pulitzer Prize, not once, but twice, for his books of poems.

There was, however, a painful detour along the way. In 1930, Warren wrote a chapter in *I'll Take My Stand*, a book of twelve controversial essays conceived primarily by four of the fugitives—Ransom, Tate, Warren, and a flinty Southern writer named Donald Davidson. The other contributors to this iconic volume, which achieved a renown far out of proportion to its actual sales, would include a novelist, a journalist, a couple of historians, a psychiatrist, and an English professor. The book took its title from a line in "Dixie," which suggested its basic purpose as well. These men (and they were all white men) set out earnestly to defend the South. The region, they felt, had been under attack, particularly from the pen of H. L. Mencken, the muckraking journalist from Baltimore, who criticized, among other things, the cultural aridity of their place.

These writers didn't care for Mencken's tone, but they had other, deeper concerns. They saw in other parts of the nation a drift—really more of a torrential rush—toward a spirit-killing materialism, which was rooted, they thought, in the industrialization that had swept across the country. The satisfaction of a hard day's work had been ripped from the nurture of God's green earth with massive damage to the human psyche and soul. But the agrarian writers of *I'll Take My Stand* saw an antidote to the problem, and it lay in the pastoral example of the South, a place where people still lived on the land with its built-in rhythms of leisure and work.

In point of fact, it should be noted, their idyllic vision of the South probably bore a greater resemblance to the Vanderbilt campus, where many of them worked, than it did to the hardscrabble farms all over the region, where white and black families were struggling to survive. This was, after all, the beginning of the Great Depression, a time of ruin in the Southern landscape. But the agrarians were poets, men of letters first of all, who thought in metaphors and dreamed of better days.

They knew in their hearts that the country was losing a piece of its soul, and even today, in these early years of the twenty-first century—a time of obsession with gadgets and things, and the runaway greed of modern corporations—the core of the agrarians' message rings true.

The problem, I think, was their jumble of intent. They set out to issue a warning to the country, delivered through a passionate defense of the South, including, unfortunately, its most dubious institution of all: racial segregation.

It fell to Robert Penn Warren to offer that defense, and at the age of twenty-five he did his best. In an essay entitled "The Briar Patch," he called for racial equality in the eyes of the law, for greater educational opportunity for Negroes (he spelled it, sadly, with a lowercase "n"), and for black and white farmers to embrace their common interests. But in 1930, he believed these goals, all worthy, could be accomplished within the framework of segregation.

By the 1950s, Warren had repudiated that view; had raised his passionate voice, in fact, in support of civil rights. But that is getting ahead of the story. In between, there was *All the King's Men*.

Warren began work on the novel, easily the best-known of his books, after taking a teaching job at Louisiana State University. He came to that handsome, oak-shaded campus in 1933, just after Huey P. Long had taken his seat as a U.S. senator. Long, who would inspire the character Willie Stark in *All the King's Men*, was one of the most remarkable politicians of his age—really, of *any* age in American history. You don't hear much about him today. There's the vague impression of a Southern demagogue, and there have been so many of those through the years that Long most often simply disappears into the dismal haze of Southern history.

The truth, however, which Robert Penn Warren understood very well, was that Huey Long was in a class by himself. He was that rarest of political figures, a left-wing radical from the South, who, if he had not been assassinated, might have been president of the United States. It would have been an uphill climb, but Long was a brilliant, charismatic politician, who offered in the depths of the Great Depression a vision of economic justice the likes of which the country had never seen. Nor has it since.

He was born in 1893 in the farming country of northern Louisiana, not quite as poor as he would try to make it sound later on. But the realities of poverty were all around. The land was hard and the timber companies had cut down the trees, and red clay gullies slashed through the hills. The people, mostly white in that particular corner of the state, scratched out a living as best they could, virtually all of them poor, though many of them were as tough as the land. In Winn Parish, where Long's family settled, they opposed secession in 1860, and some of them even fought for the Union. At the turn of the twentieth century, when Huey came along, the contrarian streak was still in full force.

He came of age with a fierce ambition to make things better; the cause of the people would be his cause—especially the poor who had suffered too long at the hands of the rich—and as he made himself their defender and champion, he would climb the ladder of Louisiana politics. From there the presidency loomed just ahead. Long had it all mapped out in his mind.

After a year at Tulane law school, he passed the bar with flying colors, and in 1918, at the age of twenty-four, he ran for his first political office. He was elected to the state Railroad Commission, a seemingly inconsequential position, but not in the hands of Huey Long. For the next six years, he worked tirelessly—some would even say ferociously—to extend railroad service to rural areas, roll back telephone rate increases, and pursue higher taxes on big corporations. In 1928 he was elected governor, and the state of Louisiana would never be the same. When Long took office, there were fewer than three hundred miles of paved roads in the state. Within two years, there were more than three thousand. He built 111 new bridges, provided free textbooks to Louisiana school children, and adopted as his campaign slogan a quote from William Jennings Bryan: "Every Man a King."

The ordinary people of Louisiana loved him, particularly the poor, who, by that time, included most of the rural population. In 1930, they elected him to the U. S. Senate, though he didn't report for duty until 1932, when he had completed his hectic term as governor and chosen a compliant, hand-picked successor. Soon after his arrival in Washington he appeared at a luncheon for Franklin D. Roosevelt, wearing a colorful suit and clashing pink tie, prompting the president's mother to whisper, "Who is that *awful* man?" Huey cheerfully returned the insult. "I like him," he said of Roosevelt. "He's not a strong man, but he means well."

As early as 1934, it was clear that Long intended to run against Roosevelt two years later, charging that the president had not done enough to end the Depression. On February 23 in a half-hour radio address to the nation, Long put forward his own plan. He called it Share Our Wealth, and though some people would question his numbers, no one could deny that the broad outlines went far beyond conventional politics. Long intended to redistribute the wealth, insisting unassailably that a tiny percentage of citizens were obscenely rich while millions of others were not sure where to find their next meal. The solution, he said, was to tax away fortunes over five million dollars, confiscating everything over eight million, with similar taxes on incomes of more than a million a year. Even the greediest tycoons, he insisted, should be satisfied with an annual compensation three hundred times the national average. The confiscated wealth would then go to the poor in the form of homeowner grants, pensions for the elderly, education grants for American students, and sharply increased benefits for veterans.

For Robert Penn Warren, watching from the vantage point of

Louisiana, it was obvious that Huey meant what he said—and even more significantly, that millions of American citizens believed him. From a literary as well as a political point of view, all of this had the makings of a powerful drama, particularly because there was another, more ominous side of the story. Whatever good Long intended to do, however serious he might be about the suffering of the poor, his thirst for power was as grand as his vision for economic justice. Indeed in Louisiana, he had used intimidation, corruption, and patronage to amass more power than any politician ever dared. The state's figure-head governor and frightened legislature passed virtually any law Long demanded, and it was a trivial measure of his lust for control that he often sat on the bench during football games and sent in the plays for LSU. The coaches knew better than to contradict him.

"Huey Long's great passion was for power and money," concluded historian Arthur Schlesinger. "These methods outweighed the good he did."

But Long's biographer, T. Harry Williams, a venerable historian at LSU, thought the story was more complicated—thought that the good and the lust for power were equal ingredients in a tragedy that ultimately ended in murder. On September 4, 1935, in a marble corridor at the Louisiana state capitol, a young Baton Rouge doctor whose father, a judge, was about to be gerrymandered out of office, waited in the shadows for Long. When the senator approached, Dr. Carl Weiss fired a single shot with a pistol, striking Long in the side before startled bodyguards opened fire, pumping thirty-two rounds into Weiss.

The doctor was killed on the spot, but Long was not. Rushed to a Baton Rouge hospital, he underwent surgery to try to stem his internal bleeding, but his damaged kidney continued to hemorrhage, and slowly, but surely Long began losing strength. After extensive interviews with those who attended the senator's bedside, T. Harry Williams, in his book, *Huey Long*, offered this account of his final hours:

At times he passed into unconsciousness and then revived and talked wildly, as though he saw visions beyond the hospital walls. He saw the people out there, the poor people of America, a mass of faces, staring at him, needing him, wanting to give him power so that he could help them . . . the one-gallus farmers of the hill lands of the South . . . the white and black sharecroppers in the broad cotton fields . . . the gaunt and debt-ridden farmers of the Great Plains . . . the unemployed factory workers tramping the streets of the Northeast . . . they looked at him and trusted him . . . and they would give him the power.

To Robert Penn Warren, all of this made an epic tale, and working off and on for the next ten years, he took the history and built a novel around it, adding more layers to a story that was already complex. By the time he finished, the book in a sense was not about Willie Stark, the fictional character based roughly on Long. Or at least Willie Stark was not the main character, which is what Hollywood never figured out in its two unsatisfying attempts at a movie. (The first attempt, with Broderick Crawford, did win an Academy Award for Best Picture, but still fell flat when compared with the book.) No, the central character in *All the King's Men* is the story's narrator, Jack Burden, a special assistant to Governor Stark, who has embarked on a turbulent journey of discovery. Willie Stark was a part of that journey. But part of it also involved falling in love, and I remember in an early reading of the book, when I was about the same age that Burden would have been, falling a little in love with Anne Stanton myself.

She was, I thought, the steadiest, sanest character in the book, and at the age of seventeen, she seemed so beautiful and so full of life. She came, like Jack, from a patrician family in south Louisiana, but hers was a part of the post-money aristocracy, her father, a former governor, having set an example of public service. Her older brother, Adam, was Jack's best friend, and would soon grow up to be a doctor, so devoted to his practice, to saving lives and doing good, that he lived an almost monastic existence. Anne herself would eventually embark on a similar path, devoting herself to charity work, but before that happened, she was a girl in love with Jack Burden, and finally one night she lay on his bed, somehow more sure of herself than Jack, whose passions were suddenly riddled with doubt.

"Anne," he whispered, ". . . it wouldn't be—it wouldn't be right."

Many years later, when the romance was over and they had both moved on, when Anne, in fact, had become the unlikely mistress of Willie Stark, Jack still carried the image in his head, tangled, he knew, with childhood memories of summers by the sea—of picnics and innocent games about to give way to something more real.

Years before, a young girl had lain there naked on the iron bed in my room with her eyes closed and her hands folded over her breast, and I had been so struck by the pathos of her submissiveness and her trust in me and of the moment which would plunge her into the full, dark stream of the world that I had hesitated before laying my hands upon her and had, without understanding myself, called out her name. At that time I had no words for what I felt, and now, too, it is difficult to find them. But lying there, she had seemed to be again the little girl who had, on the day of the picnic, floated on the waters of the bay, with her eyes closed under the stormy and grape-purple sky and the single white gull passing over, very high. As she lay there the image came into my head, and I had wanted to call her name, to tell her something—what, I did not know. She trusted me, but perhaps for that moment of hesitation I did not trust myself, and looked back upon the past as something precious about to be snatched away from us and was afraid of the future. I had not understood then what I think I have now come to understand: that we can keep the past only by having the future, for they are forever tied together.

Such was Jack Burden's flirtation with meaning, as well as with love, but for much of the book he is resistant to both, choosing to believe that "all life is but the dark heave of blood and the twitch of the nerve." The shock to Burden, as he discovers in the rush of tragedy near the end, is that there really is a meaning after all, and the pain of that truth is something with which he will have to contend.

All of this, for me, was the power and the glory of *All the King's Men*, which won the Pulitzer Prize in 1947. It was a remarkable book in so many ways—the characters, the plot, the brilliant evocation of a time and a place, and all of those things delivered in a lush and poetic prose. I'm tempted to say that Robert Penn Warren never came close to any of this again. His other novels may have had their moments, but he never found another story quite as strong. He did win two more Pulitzer Prizes for his poetry and, with Cleanth Brooks, produced two textbooks, *Understanding Poetry* and *Understanding Fiction*, that helped shape the modern study of literature. He also wrote with increasing eloquence about the civil rights movement, enlarging his understanding of equality. And there was this: among his literary peers he was widely admired for his civility and grace, his generosity of spirit. Albert Murray wrote about it in *South to a Very Old Place*, and even more colorfully, his friend Will Campbell talked about it often.

Campbell himself was an interesting character, a white Baptist preacher from south Mississippi who became a stalwart in the civil rights movement. In 1978, when he finally sat down to write about it—a memoir of his civil rights years, intertwined with the story of his big-hearted, drug-addicted, older brother, Joe—the resulting book, *Brother to a Dragonfly*, became a finalist for the National Book Award. It also won the admiration of a wide array of authors, including Robert Penn Warren.

"*Brother to a Dragonfly*," Warren wrote, "is as compelling as a fine novel, is packed with convincing characterizations, strong humor, and deep emotional appeals, and more than any single book I know tells what Southern life is like on the rough side, where the lath and plaster have not been smoothed off, including matters of daily bread, race, and the belief in Jesus Christ."

It was hard to say which of these writers admired the other more. But Campbell, who plied his literary trade in a three-room cabin outside of Nashville, loved to tell the story of a visit that Warren once made to his place. "Yep," he said with a mischievous grin, "ol' Red Warren—I called him Red—was sure quite a talker. He sat right there in that very chair. The one you're sitting in right now. And let me show you something else." Campbell led me out the back door of the cabin and gestured toward a large flat boulder half hidden in the weeds.

"You see that rock? The one right there? That's a very historic spot. There probably ought to be a marker or something. Ol' Red Warren peed on that very rock."

II

I remember how, in that same conversation, Campbell talked a long time about *All the King's Men*, and why one book stands out above another. He mentioned Faulkner and Walker Percy, and how they both had that Southern sense of place, and we tried to think of other writers, not from the South, who were able to evoke the same kind of feeling. I remember that I mentioned two books, Peter Matthiessen's often overlooked novel, *At Play in the Fields of the Lord*, and David Guterson's *Snow Falling on Cedars*—both of which, for whatever personal and complicated reasons, rank right there for me with *All the King's Men*. Both authors, certainly, have a gift for the language. In Matthiessen's case, it's been honed over the course of a colorful career that has led him to the distant corners of the earth. As a young writer in the 1950s, he made the obligatory journey to Paris, much like James Baldwin or Ernest Hemingway, and there in 1953 he was a founding editor of the *Paris Review*.

After that, his travels began in earnest. Between the 1950s and the early years of the twenty-first century, Matthiessen explored the far reaches of Alaska, Australia, and South America, and later Antarctica, New Guinea, and Tibet. Most of his twenty-two works of nonfiction, including his best-known book, *The Snow Leopard*, are based on those travels. And so, in fact, are some of his novels. *At Play in the Fields of the Lord* is a story set in the Amazon jungle, a land overflowing with violence and life—like some kind of Eden, many writers have noted, and Matthiessen did not disagree:

> . . . *the morning light was vague and luminous, sepulchral, like the light in a dark cathedral; the brown-greeniness of the atmosphere was so tactile that he could rub it between his fingertips. The forest life went on far overhead, in the green galleries; it was only in the sun space cleared by death and fall that new life could rise out of the forest floor. Beneath his feet the ground was not ground at all, but a dark compost of slow seepings and rotted leaves which, starved of sun, reared nothing but low fungi; it gave off a thick, bitter smell of acid.*

A few years after first reading that description, I, too, made a trip to the Amazon jungle, flying out across the unbroken forest in a small bush plane. The pilot tried to be reassuring.

"This plane," he said, "is specially made for jungle flying. It'll fly very slow, so we can land in any kind of clearing. And if it were to crash we'd probably survive. The metal is reinforced."

"That's good," I said.

"Not that good," replied the pilot. "As you can see we're flying over very dense jungle. If we crashed we'd land in the top of the canopy, and these trees are two hundred feet tall. There would be no way to get down.

"Welcome to the Amazon," he added.

Already in awe of its unfamiliarity, I had come to the jungle on a newspaper assignment, a story on a group of missionaries who had set out on an unlikely quest—to translate the Bible into every language on earth. They worked for an organization called the Southern Institute of Linguistics, which had, in its first forty years of existence, begun translations in more than seven hundred dialects. Most of those were previously unwritten, and thus the cultural implications were startling. For better or worse, these particular missionaries were bestowing upon hundreds of remote and primitive cultures the awesome gift of a written language—the rough anthropological equivalent, you could argue, of the wheel, or maybe even fire.

I had come to observe their work in Peru, stopping first in the tiny village of Aguachini where the Andes Mountains gave way to the jungle, and where some of the people in the Ashenica tribe had never seen a white person before. There was a small landing strip in a clearing near the village, a place where visitors came so seldom that the grass was nearly eight feet tall. But David Payne had been there before. Payne was twenty-six years old, a tall and shaggy-haired missionary-linguist who reminded me more of a Peace Corps volunteer. He had a deep

respect for the people of the jungle, admiring the gentleness of a culture in a place where life could be so hard. He understood that one
of the most common words in the Ashenica language was *nonashitaro*,
which means "to suffer," and like many others who respected its past
he also feared for the future of the tribe.

The outside world was closing in quickly, lured of course by the
prospect of wealth—by oil and precious metals and timber—and by
an ethic of exploitation and greed; a world view leaving little room for
worry over cultural or ecological disaster. Against this reality, David
Payne held fast to an article of faith, or at least to a hope, that his work
was helping jungle people to prepare. If they could read and write—
and if, in addition, they could secure a written title to their land, and
build their own health clinics and schools, and if they understood the
workings of the world bearing down—perhaps, somehow, they could
fortify themselves for a collision that everybody knew was coming.

The key, Payne believed, was a literacy rooted in their own written language, and a cultural identity that went along with it, and thus
he was deeply committed to his mission. He understood, however,
that it could be double-edged. The critics of the Southern Institute
of Linguistics saw it not as a buffer for the jungle Indians, but simply
as the first wave of development—an advance team for the forces of
greed who tore at the heart of the tribal way of life. For some of these
Indians, their departure from the Stone Age was easy to measure—a
machete, perhaps, or an aluminum pot. Otherwise, the ancient ways
survived, but were fragile in the face of Christian theology, or even
the simple notion that germs, and not evil spirits, caused the Indian
people to get sick. In the massive cultural confusion that followed,
the indigenous tribes became easy prey for an oil or timber company
that wanted their land.

In the broadest sense, this is what Matthiessen's novel is about—the collision of cultures in the Amazon Basin in which the Indians, inevitably, are the losers. But the story, not surprisingly, is more complex. Matthiessen has a gift for creating character, for using dialogue and point of view to bring unfamiliar figures to life—a missionary struggling to understand his own faith; a missionary's wife, slowly falling out of love with her husband; a soldier of fortune, wrestling with his American Indian boyhood; the dignified chief of a wild jungle tribe, trying to lead his troubled people through their first encounter with the outside world.

It is easy to imagine in a setting such as this that the story would crackle with adventure and violence, which it does. But for me at least, the unforgettable brilliance of Matthiessen's novel was that it was driven more by character than plot—by the spiritual quests of Boronai and Lewis Moon, the sexual longings of the girl, Andy Huben, and by a missionary's loss of faith, not in God, but in his own faith.

In the jungle, during one night in each month, the moths did not come to lanterns; through the black reaches of the outer night, so it was said, they flew toward the full moon.

So it was said. He could not recall where he had heard it, or from whom; it had been somewhere on the rivers of Brazil. He had never watched the lanterns at the time of the full moon; when he remembered it was always the dark of the moon or beyond the tropics. Yet the idea of the moths in the high darkness, straining upward, filled him with longing, and at these times he would know that he had not found what he was looking for, nor come closer to discovering what it was.

Through this powerful evocation of place, Peter Matthiessen, like all great writers, sets off on a journey through the human condition, and so, in his own way, does David Guterson in *Snow Falling on Ce-*

dars. Though his setting is different, a fishing village on Puget Sound, Guterson uses character as deftly as Matthiessen and history with the power of Robert Penn Warren.

Before I read *Snow Falling on Cedars* the history at the heart of its story had never had a face. I remember feeling a vague discomfort when I learned of Japanese internment camps, wondering how, even in the middle of World War II, the United States could do such a thing. We were, after all, the land of the free. The numbers alone were unsettling enough—110,000 Japanese Americans, most of whom were born in this country, rounded up and taken away to the camps; but it was not until 1994, with the publication of this novel, that I began to think about what really happened.

It was not the only time, of course, that a novelist had accomplished what historians couldn't; Kurt Vonnegut had done the same in *Slaughterhouse-Five,* had seen the literary power in glossed-over history, and so had Warren in *All the King's Men.* And now here was Guterson, sketching the hysteria after Pearl Harbor, the shock and the rage that swept through the country—and specifically, in this case, through an island community on Puget Sound, dividing whites and Japanese Americans, all of them sons and daughters of immigrants. Soon after the attack, an order came from the U.S. War Relocation Authority: all islanders of Japanese descent had eight days to get ready to move. They were taken away on a slow-moving train, a scene vaguely reminiscent of those unfolding in Europe as the S.S. forces rounded up the Jews. There was one major difference, of course. No gas chambers awaited the Japanese; there was instead, for this group of prisoners, a single square mile in the Mojave Desert.

The bitter wind came down off the mountains and through the barbed wire and hurled the desert sand in their faces. The camp was only half-finished;

there were not enough barracks to go around. Some people, on arriving, had to build their own in order to have a place to sleep. There were crowds everywhere, thousands of people in a square mile of desert scoured to dust by army bulldozers, and there was nowhere for a person to find solitude. The barracks all looked the same . . . On the fourth night a young man in Barrack 17 shot his wife and then himself while they lay in bed together—somehow he had smuggled in a gun. "Shikata ga nai," people said. "It cannot be helped."

It was not the first time—and certainly not the last—that fear would take its toll on the American psyche, and a generation later President Reagan issued an apology for the nation. Signing a resolution passed by Congress, he acknowledged a moment of national shame, rooted, he said, in "race prejudice, war hysteria, and a failure of political leadership."

If *Snow Falling on Cedars* captures the reality of that time, it is, in the end, more than a novel about the wounds of war. It is also a story of love, tender and star-crossed, and of a community struggling to do the right thing after a Japanese American is accused of murder. As the characters in the novel come vividly to life, perhaps the most intriguing is Hatsue Imada, a Japanese American girl searching through her own multilayered identity—the deeply held traditions of her family, her love of a boy who was not Japanese, her love of the sea and the cedar-shrouded island on which she was born: this tiny microcosm in the heart of Puget Sound where the passions of war were tearing neighbors apart. For Hatsue all of these complications receded only in the deep island forests, a place she had shared with her lover, Ishmael, and which beckoned to her when she was most alone.

Deep among the trees she lay on a fallen log and gazed far up branchless trunks. A late winter wind blew the tops around, inducing in her a momentary vertigo. She admired a Douglas fir's complicated bark, followed its grooves to the canopy of branches two hundred feet above. The world was incomprehensibly intricate, and yet this forest made a simple sense in her heart that she felt nowhere else.

Such was the poetry of Guterson's prose, the sensuality, history and strong sense of place, which, for me at least, put him in the company of Matthiessen and Warren. I have returned to each of these books many times, driven, in part, by a case of writer's envy, but more than that by the lure of the truth—by a sense of simple beauty in the world and the terrible complexity of the heart.

· 8 ·

Forgotten Histories

FEATURING:

The Grapes of Wrath—John Steinbeck

Bury My Heart at Wounded Knee—Dee Brown

ALSO, WOODY GUTHRIE, MERLE HAGGARD,
CAREY MCWILLIAMS, KRIS KRISTOFFERSON,
BRUCE SPRINGSTEEN, VINE DELORIA JR.

I

IT WAS ALWAYS a hard way of life and Woody Guthrie sang about it all. When he was a boy, his father had told him about a lynching, how he had been there, had been a part of it, and how one of those dangling from the bridge was a woman—a black woman, he said, and she was mean; tried to kill the sheriff before they took her away, and her son was there and he was mean, too, and finally they got what was coming to them. It happened on an Oklahoma afternoon, and there were photographs that somebody took; later made them into a post card, and that was how Laura Nelson and her boy went down in history, hanging side by side above the river.

Woody wrote three songs about it, about his Klansman father and this bitter land in which he was raised, but he also knew there was more to the story—more to the land and the people who coaxed a hard living from it before it finally gave way to the dust. Woody was born in 1912, a luckless son of the southern plains when people still thought they could turn it into farms. For a while the rains fell steady and strong, especially as the first dirt farmers came and plowed away the deep prairie grasses that had always held fast to the soil. The men plowed their fields in long, straight rows and their cotton crops stole nutrients from the earth, and finally in the summer of 1930 the rains went away. Month after month, year after year, the land grew dry and the hard prairie winds carried clouds of dust all the way to the Atlantic.

On April 14, 1935, winds of sixty miles an hour descended on the plains and stirred a mountain of dust so high it blotted out the sun. The prairie people called the day "Black Sunday." Not long after, Woody Guthrie wrote a song called "Black Pneumonia" about that day and a few others like it: about people getting sick when they tried to breathe. Woody was living in Texas then, in a Panhandle town just across the state line, and like thousands of his neighbors in that part of the West—in Texas, New Mexico, Kansas, South Dakota, but most of all in Oklahoma—he set off in search of better times.

Many of the Okies, as they were then known, wound up in California, flooding the migrant labor camps and sometimes working for starvation wages. Woody, for his part, kept writing songs, kept trying to tell the story of hard times, for he was a "small-c" communist, flirting with the theories of Karl Marx, and writing tribute songs to Pretty Boy Floyd, Franklin Roosevelt, and Jesus Christ—to people

who seemed to care about the poor. But mostly he wrote about ordinary folks, and his most famous song, "This Land Is Your Land,"
proclaimed a my-country-too kind of patriotism, offering the radical
affirmation that America belonged to its working people as much as
it belonged to the rich.

A generation later another Dust Bowl poet came along, or rather a
poet of the Okie refugees who had suffered oppression in California,
pushed to the point almost of giving up. This is the way Merle Haggard told the story:

> *I remember daddy praying for a better way of life*
> *But I don't recall a change of any size*
> *Just a little loss of courage as their age began to show*
> *And more sadness in my mama's hungry eyes.*

These were artists who tried to put into words the dark underside
of the American story, the disillusionment at the hands of a country
they loved, and they did it in bursts of poetry and feeling. As they tried
to make the story come alive, they knew with certainty and deep gratitude that they were not alone. There was also John Steinbeck, whose
iconic novel, *The Grapes of Wrath*, became a centerpiece in the telling.

Steinbeck was born in Salinas, California, a point of destination
for the Okies, and as a young but well-established writer in the 1930s,
he saw the misery taking shape all around. It was a human tragedy;
that much was clear—all these people driven by calamity from their
homes, hoping to start again in California, to find a piece of fertile
land and to help make it bloom. They didn't mind picking another
man's crops, whether cotton or grapes, cauliflower or lettuce; for a
while at least it would be all right, for they would work hard and put
a little money aside and pretty soon they would have their own place.

They could see when they crossed the last mountain range that there were still vast acres waiting for the plow.

Soon, however, they discovered something else. There were simply too many refugees, too many people scrambling for jobs and driving down wages almost to the point that it didn't pay to work. But they had to work, for what else could they do, assuming they were lucky enough to get the jobs. In 1936, John Steinbeck, who had studied journalism at Stanford University, accepted an assignment from the *San Francisco News* to write a series of articles about the Okies. He enlisted the aid of a federal bureaucrat by the name of Tom Collins, a thinnish man with high cheekbones and a little mustache and a look of kindness deep in his eyes. Collins was director of a migrant labor camp in Kern County, California, a New Deal experiment that became a study in grassroots democracy.

In the Kern County camp, the migrants mostly governed themselves. Paying rent of a dollar a week, they elected a Central Committee to make the camp rules, and those families too broke to pay any rent worked it off by doing maintenance chores in the camp. The workers policed the grounds themselves, and the local and state police of California, who were developing a reputation for brutality, were not allowed in the camp without a warrant. As federal administrator of the facility, Collins understood that it was a far cry from conditions elsewhere, and as he and Steinbeck set off on a tour of the state, the stark realities came quickly into focus. As Steinbeck wrote in the *San Francisco News*, "In California we find a curious attitude toward a group that makes our agriculture successful. They are needed and they are hated."

The hatred was an institutional thing, Steinbeck concluded, a mixture of bigotry and economics. In "The Harvest Gypsies," his seven-part newspaper account, he set out to explain how it worked.

For generations, he noted, agriculture in California had been unlike anything the Dust Bowl refugees had ever seen. In California, farming was a business, not the product of one man's sweat or love of the soil, but a corporate undertaking with decisions made in distant boardrooms. The faceless people who ran these vast farms knew they had a ready supply of labor—tenant farmers whose lives had come apart in Oklahoma, who had made the crossing to California, starting out with almost nothing, watching children die along the way, or perhaps grandparents too old to start again; and they struggled to keep old cars running and old tires patched, and when they finally made it to the promised land, they were almost always broke. So they took whatever jobs they could find, in a peach orchard maybe with two thousand others, and bought food on credit at the corporate store, and pretty soon they were working for no money at all, toiling simply to pay off debt. Then the peaches were picked and the workers moved on, settling most often in squatters' camps, building huts of scraps from the garbage dump, and their bellies were empty and their eyes were glazed with desperation and hurt.

"The workers are herded about like animals," Steinbeck wrote. "Every possible method is used to make them feel inferior and insecure. At the slightest suspicion that the men are organizing they are run from the ranch at the points of guns. The large ranch owners know that if organization is ever effected there will be the expense of toilets, showers, decent living conditions and a raise in wages."

And so the situation grew worse. Sometimes smallpox descended on the camps, wiping out whole families, or children died from too little food, leaving their parents, as Steinbeck put it, with "that paralyzed dullness with which the mind protects itself against too much pain." But perhaps the most bitter image of all came in the winter of 1938. Two years after his newspaper series, with the migrant story still tearing at his conscience, Steinbeck drove to the town of Visalia, where the rain had fallen for nearly three weeks. He was there on assignment for *Life* magazine, and the scene of misery and disease left his objectivity in shreds.

"The water is a foot deep in the tents," he wrote, "and the children are up on the beds and there is no food and no fire, and the county has taken off all the nurses because 'the problem is so great we can't do anything about it.' So they do nothing."

It was apparently that experience that propelled him to write *The Grapes of Wrath*, to move beyond his journalistic efforts, and even his first attempt at a novel, to write something more ambitious, more disturbing and grand. Writing in longhand, as he always did, he began to craft a scene about the flood:

The rain began with gusty showers, pauses and downpours; and then gradually it settled to a single tempo, small drops and a steady beat, rain that was gray to see through, rain that cut midday light to evening. And at first the dry earth . . . drank the rain, until the earth was full. Then puddles formed, and in the low places little lakes formed in the fields. The muddy lakes rose higher, and the steady rain whipped the shining water. At last the mountains were full, and the hillsides spilled into the streams, built them to freshets, and sent them roaring down the canyons into the valleys . . . Level fields became lakes, broad and gray . . .

Steinbeck knew, by 1938, that the story needed an artist's touch—the literary equivalent of Woody Guthrie's songs, or perhaps of Dorothea Lange's photographs. He had worked with Lange, a photographer living in Berkeley, on his articles for the *San Francisco News*, and it was easy to feel the power of her art. There was one image in particular that stood out from the rest, a photograph taken in 1936 that came to be known as "The Migrant Mother." The woman in the picture, Florence Owens Thompson, looks much older than her thirty-two years, with two small children huddled beside her and her face a mixture of desperation and pride.

"I saw and approached the hungry and desperate mother, as if drawn by a magnet," Lange later recalled. "I do not remember how I explained my presence or my camera to her, but I do remember she asked me no questions. I made five exposures, working closer and closer from the same direction. I did not ask her name or her history. She told me her age, that she was thirty-two. She said that they had been living on frozen vegetables from the surrounding fields, and birds that the children killed. She had just sold the tires from her car to buy food. There she sat in that lean-to tent with her children huddled around her, and seemed to know that my pictures might help her, and so she helped me. There was a sort of equality about it."

There were some who compared the force of the photograph to the early paintings of Vincent Van Gogh, when he grew fascinated by the miners of Belgium and the peasants of Holland, helping to shift the focus of art from the realm of kings to the pain and nobility of ordinary people. Fifty years later, Steinbeck was driven by the same sense of mission.

"The writer can only write about what he admires," Steinbeck declared. "Present day kings aren't very inspiring, the gods are on vacation . . . and since our race admires gallantry, the writer will deal with it where he finds it. He finds it in the struggling poor . . ."

As he began to write, there were moments he feared he couldn't carry it off. "I'm not a writer," he confessed in his diary. "I've been fooling myself and other people." But then the words began to flow, coming in a torrent of two thousand a day, and by the fall of 1938 he was finished. His wife, Carol, had suggested a title from "The Battle

Hymn of the Republic," and somehow that phrase, "the grapes of wrath," had given him an edge, a final sense of focus for a story that he thought could be extraordinary.

When the novel was published on April 14, 1939—the fourth anniversary of the "Black Sunday" dust storm in Oklahoma—the public reaction confirmed his hopes, as well as some of his fears. Sales the first year topped four hundred thousand (on the way to fifteen million by the end of the century); there were more than one hundred and fifty reviews, most of which were positive; and Steinbeck won the Pulitzer Prize. But there were also detractors, especially on the political right. An Oklahoma congressman called the book "a lie, a black, infernal creation of a twisted, distorted mind," and as Steinbeck scholar Robert DeMott has noted, California agribusiness leaders "mounted smear campaigns to discredit the book and its author."

As of this writing, the debate has raged for more than seventy years. In 2002 conservative critic Keith Windschuttle insisted, ". . . almost everything about the elaborate picture created in the novel is either outright false or exaggerated beyond belief." But the more liberal Norman Mailer, a gifted novelist in his own right, seemed to speak for the critical majority when he declared: "I wonder if any of us since have been equal to Steinbeck's marvelous and ironic sense of compassion . . . What a great novel was *The Grapes of Wrath.*"

Among other things, Mailer shared the admiration many others felt for the risks that Steinbeck took as a writer—his willingness to travel, as Mailer put it, "to the very abyss of offering more feeling than the reader can accept." Steinbeck did it with a unique structure, alternating chapters about the Joads, a fictional family fleeing the devastations of the Dust Bowl, with broader, more lyrical descriptions of a history unfolding even as he wrote.

The houses were left vacant on the land, and the land was vacant because of this. Only the tractor sheds of corrugated iron, silver and gleaming, were alive; and they were alive with metal and gasoline and oil, the disks of the plows shining. The tractors had lights shining, for there is no day and night for a tractor and the disks turn the earth in the darkness and they glitter in the daylight. And when a horse stops work and goes into the barn there is a life and a vitality left, there is a breathing and a warmth, and the feet shift on the straw, and the jaws champ on the hay, and the ears and the eyes are alive. There is a warmth of life in the barn, and the heat and smell of life. But when the motor of a tractor stops, it is as dead as the ore it came from.

What Steinbeck was saying in this rush of poetry, this torrent of feeling that became his book, was that the natural and economic disasters, bad as they were, were not the full story of *The Grapes of Wrath*. There was also the loss of something fundamental, as the love of the land gave way to simple greed and farms became agricultural factories, and the goal of the owners was to hold down costs, no matter the level of human suffering and pain. Humanity itself was threatened in the process—the workers' certainly, but the owners' also, for in their hunger for profit and wealth they were stripping the nobility from their own lives. Indeed, as Steinbeck understood the story, only the desperate workers in the fields, the families huddled in disease-riddled camps, managed to keep simple decency alive. In *The Grapes of Wrath*, the decency was there, ironically, in the character of Tom Joad, a paroled and unrepentant killer working with his friend, Jim Casy, a fallen preacher, to organize the migrants.

"Wherever they's a fight so hungry people can eat, I'll be there," Joad proclaims, in perhaps the most famous passage in the book. "Wherever they's a cop beatin' up a guy, I'll be there."

But it wasn't just Tom, the central protagonist, who embodied the heroism of the novel. Throughout the story his mother, Ma Joad, works fiercely to hold her family together, and his younger sister, Rose of Sharon, when her baby is stillborn, offers her breast to a starving stranger, knowing that otherwise he will die. And when Steinbeck's editors found the scene too erotic—too startling and melodramatic to be believed—he resolutely refused to take it out. "I think I know how I want it," he said. "And if I'm wrong, I'm alone in my wrongness."

Wayne Flynt, an Alabama historian who has written at length about the Depression, believes that Steinbeck avoided a trap that was common among even the best of writers. The characters in *The Grapes of Wrath*, he noted, were poor and white, a class of people who have not fared well in American fiction. "From the Southwestern humorists to Harper Lee," Flynt wrote, "poor whites appear as an object of satire and scorn, characterized by shiftlessness, racism, violence and demagoguery. Perhaps every society feels compelled to rationalize to itself the presence of so many poor people. What better way than to depict them as receiving what they deserve, suffering the consequences of their own failure . . ."

One of the unrelenting missions of *The Grapes of Wrath* was to make such rationalizations impossible, and Steinbeck did it without apology. Nor was he alone. Carey McWilliams, a California journalist who would later become editor of the *Nation*, published his own best seller in 1939. His book, *Factories in the Field*, was a blend of sociology, history and journalism, tracing the evolution of California agriculture from the days of the Gold Rush through the Depression: a ninety-year span that included, as McWilliams made clear, the continuous oppression of workers in the fields. In the earliest days, those workers most often were American Indians, replaced in succession by Chinese, Japanese, Mexicans and Filipinos before the coming of the Dust Bowl refugees.

In the twentieth-century economy of California, the corporate farmers recruited more workers than they could employ, thus driving down wages in a contrived and frantic competition for jobs. Not surprisingly, McWilliams reported, confirming Steinbeck's novelistic portrait, living conditions were often appalling, migrants living in camps, often in tents, with no running water, and in the prevailing mythology of the time the filth was blamed on the workers themselves. In 1936, a publicist for the California growers described field hands as "the most worthless, unscrupulous, shiftless, diseased, semi-barbarian that has ever come to our shores."

For a seven-year period beginning in 1929, the workers fought back. A wave of strikes rippled through the valleys, as migrants demanded better wages and safer, more sanitary places to live. The response most often was vigilante violence. According to McWilliams, California strikebreakers in the 1930s employed a combination of beatings, cross-burnings, and sometimes murder to intimidate workers. And yet the refugees kept coming, kept heading west, driven by drought and dust and the lure of good land. In the end, McWilliams's journalistic portrayal was as stark and disturbing as Steinbeck's novel, and the two books' appearance within the same year reinforced the credibility of both. Both became best sellers, but it was *The Grapes of Wrath* that became iconic.

In 1940 John Ford directed an Academy Award-winning film, an adaptation of the novel, ending on a note of bravery and hope. Ma Joad, played in the movie by Oscar winner Jane Darwell, delivers this summation of her family's troubles:

I ain't never gonna be scared no more. I was, though. For a while it looked as though we was beat. Good and beat. Looked like we didn't have nobody in the whole wide world but enemies. Like nobody was friendly no more. Made me feel kinda bad and scared too, like we was lost and nobody cared . . . but we keep on coming. We're the people that live. They can't wipe us out, they can't lick us. We'll go on forever, Pa, cos we're the people.

Woody Guthrie, among others, was ecstatic after he saw the movie, thrilled with the portrayal of strength that it offered, for he had been a part of that strength. He, too, had been driven from his home in Oklahoma, had written his songs about the Dust Bowl journey, and now he wrote another that he called "Tom Joad." *Wherever men are fightin' for their rights, that's where I'm a-gonna be, Ma. That's where I'm a-gonna be.*

In the torrent of art that Steinbeck inspired, Guthrie was merely the first of the twentieth century's finest songwriters to write directly about *The Grapes of Wrath*. A generation later, Kris Kristofferson wrote "Here Comes That Rainbow Again," a bit of poetry adapted from the story of the Joads' journey west. In the book they stop at a desert café with hunger setting in and their money running low, and they plead with the waitress for a loaf of bread—not as charity, not as a gift, but as something they could buy for a dime. The waitress sells them the bread and then sees the Joad children, Ruthie and Winfield, eyeing a container of nickel candy. "Them's two for a penny," she says. In his song, released in 1981, Kristofferson offers this chorus to punctuate the story:

And the daylight grew heavy with thunder,
and the smell of the rain on the wind.
Ain't it just like a human.
Here comes that rainbow again.

What Kristofferson saw clearly in *The Grapes of Wrath*, embedded in the massive story of despair, was a kind of existential triumph, a humanity that was stronger than social injustice. That seemed to be the general impression of the artists—Kristofferson, John Ford, Woody Guthrie—and later Bruce Springsteen, who, in 1995, crafted an album called "The Ghost of Tom Joad," an echo of hope in hard times.

> *Waitin' for when the last shall be first and the first shall be last*
> *In a cardboard box 'neath the underpass.*

Oddly enough, some of these songs prompted my return to *The Grapes of Wrath*, to a reconsideration of its artistry and meaning, and the multiple layers of Steinbeck's achievement. Until then the novel had mostly been a revelation, light shone on a darkened corner of history, about which I knew nothing at all.

II

It was late high school when I came upon the legacy of John Steinbeck. I loved his words and was deeply moved by the story of the Joads, and since this was a novel I assumed at first that the author had simply made the whole thing up. No, my English teacher explained; Steinbeck's story was rooted in the truth. I remember my astonishment at this bit of knowledge. I knew about social injustice, of course, but mostly in the South, and I knew a little about the Great Depression and the alphabet soup of New Deal programs. But it had never occurred to me that greed had run with so little shame through the idyllic countryside of California.

Looking back on it now, I can think of only one other book that had a similar impact on my notion of history, particularly the history of our own country. That book, *Bury My Heart at Wounded Knee*, was very different from *The Grapes of Wrath*—different subject matter, a work of nonfiction instead of a novel, but the poetic force was remarkably the same. Dee Brown, like Steinbeck before him, had entered the world of history's losers, and his empathetic journey was, if anything, even more unexpected.

Brown was such an unlikely candidate to force a basic reconsideration of our history—of the conquest of American Indians and the expansion of a country across the breadth of a continent. Until *Bury My Heart*, which was published in 1970, it was a story told almost exclusively by the winners. Like many others, I thought when I read this passionate book that Brown must be an American Indian, for how else could he have felt so deeply the tragedy at the heart of the white man's triumph? I was astonished to discover that he was, in fact, a white librarian from Arkansas.

It was a measure of the originality of his work, and the strength of his writing, that almost everyone found it disturbing. The latter-day defenders of Manifest Destiny called it one-sided, which of course it was. Brown made no apology for that. He was, after all, setting out in a single book to balance the scales on a century's worth of history—a national understanding in which Indians were, as Brown put it, "the dark menace of the myths."

In refuting that notion, Brown relied on primary sources—particularly the rich record of negotiation between the Indians and the U.S. government. As a librarian he knew his way around these musty troves of revelation, and as a novelist-turned-historian he also knew how to tell a good story. His principal instrument in *Bury My Heart* was simply to adopt the Indians' point of view, to refer, for example, to the month of October as the Falling Leaves Moon or December as the Moon When the Wolves Run Together. He also offered a ready supply of villains. There was, for example, Colonel John Chivington, a barrel-chested cavalry commander who on November 29, 1864, led a force of volunteers against a peaceful village of Cheyenne and Arapaho, camped at Sand Creek in the eastern part of Colorado. In the carnage that followed, Chivington's soldiers killed and mutilated more than one hundred Indians, mostly women and children. They carried away scalps, genitalia, and other body parts as souvenirs, and even at the time many people were appalled.

"Jis to think of that dog Chivington and his dirty hounds, up thar at Sand Creek," declared the Indian fighter Kit Carson. "His men shot down squaws, and blew the brains out of little innocent children. You call sich soldiers Christians, do ye? And Indians savages? What der yer 'spose our Heavenly Father, who made both them and us, thinks of these things?"

In *Bury My Heart at Wounded Knee*, Dee Brown follows the exploits of Colonel Chivington, and also of General Phillip Sheridan, famous for the phrase, "The only good Indian is a dead Indian." (Actually, according to Brown, what Sheridan really said was "The only good Indians I ever saw were dead." The general's words, written down by one of his lieutenants, were passed along and polished through the years.) And of course we meet George Armstrong Custer, known to the Indians as Long Hair and also as Hard Backside for his apparent willingness to ride for days in pursuit of a fight. From the Native American point of view—with the conspicuous exception of Custer's Last Stand—most of these encounters with the army ended badly, leading at last to Wounded Knee.

The wintry dusk and the tiny crystals of ice dancing in the dying light added a supernatural quality to the somber landscape. Somewhere along the frozen stream the heart of Crazy Horse lay in a secret place, and the Ghost Dancers believed that his disembodied spirit was waiting impatiently for the new earth that would surely come with the first green grass of spring.

On this particular day, December 28, 1890, a band of Hunkpapa and Minneconjou Sioux had been taken to Wounded Knee by troops from the Seventh U.S. Cavalry. It was the same unit, reconstituted, that had been led to its bloody demise by Custer. Now, fourteen years after Little Big Horn, many of the soldiers thirsted for revenge. At the very least, they seemed to relish their current assignment, which was essentially an exercise in humiliation. They were under orders to disarm this peaceful band of Sioux, a defeated people, by taking away their last hunting rifles. All over the West, tribes that had once roamed freely through the plains were now confined to reservations, tiny remnants of their vast homelands, but a few had discovered a glimmer of hope—a desperate consolation against poverty and despair—in the contagious teachings of a Paiute prophet. This prophet, Wakova, spoke of a day not far in the future when the prairie grass would once again turn green, and the buffalo and the fallen ancestors, who now roamed the hunting grounds as ghosts, would return together, and the Indian people would live in peace.

Soon, the believers in every tribe began to dance the Ghost Dance, and once again the white people were afraid. They called on the soldiers to end this madness, to take away the last remaining rifles before the Indians, in their delirium, were stirred to revolt. Thus, on the morning of December 29, the Sioux at Wounded Knee were ordered to give up their guns. One young brave named Black Coyote raised his rifle above his head in defiance, and the soldiers immediately opened fire. Within a few minutes nearly three hundred Indians, the majority of them women and children, lay dead or dying in the South Dakota snow. Brown ended his account, the final pages of his heart-breaking book, with the words of Black Elk, a Wounded Knee survivor:

I did not know then how much was ended. When I look back now from this high hill of my old age, I can still see the butchered women and children lying heaped and scattered all along the crooked gulch as plain as when I saw them with eyes still young. And I can see that something else died there in the bloody mud, and was buried in the blizzard. A people's dream died there. It was a beautiful dream . . .

Among many others, Vine Deloria Jr., a Sioux author whose "Indian Manifesto," *Custer Died for Your Sins*, was a simultaneous best seller with *Bury My Heart*, was deeply moved by the power of Brown's book. "A magnificent work," he proclaimed. "The real story of the settling of the West—the Indian side of the ledger . . . Every Indian will be happy to read this book—and will wish *he* had written it. I wish I had."

I'm not an Indian, but I understood exactly what Deloria was saying. Having also read *Custer Died for Your Sins*, I felt as readers in 1939 must have felt after reading Steinbeck and Carey McWilliams. Here was a story I simply hadn't known, a shameful history of atrocity and greed, and a way of life that had been overrun. As a young reporter in the 1970s, thoroughly inspired by Deloria and Brown, I spent the early part of my career also writing about Native Americans—not their history so much as the problems they faced in the twentieth century.

From the Everglades to the Wind River Mountains, from North Carolina to the northern Cascades, I began to interview Indian people and the story that slowly began to emerge seemed no longer to be one of despair. It was true that massive problems remained. Poverty was the norm on most reservations, and with it the lingering echo of defeat. Suicide was a leading cause of death among the young. And yet there was also a kind of renaissance, uncertain at first, but rooted, I thought, in a newfound sense of identity and pride. It would be an oversimplification to give the credit for that to Dee Brown. But traveling from one reservation to another, it was absolutely clear to me what he and Vine Deloria had wrought. They had not only rewritten the history of the West, but had also reaffirmed what it meant to be an Indian—the spirituality and love of the land, the willingness to live in harmony with nature; qualities that society as a whole would do well to adopt.

Most obviously, of course, these writers—like Steinbeck before them—offered an affirmation of humanity in the face of its opposite, a discovery embedded in the agony of events that sometimes only the artist can see.

· 9 ·

Family Values

FEATURING:

Roots—Alex Haley

Ava's Man—Rick Bragg

The Great Santini—Pat Conroy

ALSO, C. ERIC LINCOLN, TIM MCLAURIN, HARRY CREWS, TIM RUSSERT, CALVIN TRILLIN, WINSTON GROOM

I

I CAME FROM a family with a patriarch. My grandfather, Samuel Palmer Gaillard, was ninety years old when I was born, and lived to be 103, and told me stories about the Civil War. I came to think of him as the family *griot*, a term I learned from Alex Haley, and it was a role he passed along to his daughters. They, too, became keepers of the family myth, that body of knowledge and understanding that one generation, if it is wise enough, has the opportunity to pass along to the next. In our family there were stories of the Revolutionary War and the family's journey to the Alabama frontier; of the California Gold Rush, and the Apache chief Geronimo on a prison train passing through Mobile; of my grandfather's memory of that Indian face: not the ferocity that he had expected, but a sadness haunting dark, furtive eyes.

All of this was part of an oral history passed down carefully through the years, until in 1988 my Aunt Mary—the last of the family storytellers—died. For me, the most cherished part of her inheritance was a cardboard box. In it I found deeds and letters and certificates of baptism, a kind of treasure trove of confirmation that the oral histories I had learned were the truth. There were certainly embellishments here and there, the prerogatives of a good storyteller, but somehow as I sifted through the contents of the box, the people I had heard about in the stories became more fully alive. And the most remarkable thing was this: in their letters especially, they spoke in a language I knew very well. I heard my grandfather's voice in theirs, and my father's, perhaps even my own, and I set about creating a gift for my daughters—a book that would chronicle for Rachel and Tracy a family's journey through the mists of Southern history.

As I began to work on the project, the writer I thought about most was Alex Haley, the author of *Roots*, that iconic account of another family's journey. I don't mean to say that I ever thought I could equal Haley's feat. But I did find a measure of inspiration in what he had left us, in the way he embodied as fully as any writer I know that universal need to know where we came from—to connect our own story to something even larger, and thus to enrich it. That was the remarkable thing about *Roots*. In lesser hands it could have been an African American story and nothing more, and there would have been no shame in that. It was important enough for later generations who may have pushed it aside to learn the story of the middle passage, when the newly kidnapped slaves-to-be lived for months in the darkened hold of a ship, shackled and chained and tossed by the waves, stacked together on coarse wooden shelves, where they could not stand up, where they ate rancid food and often lay in their own waste until, inevitably, some died.

It would have been enough to relearn all of that. But Haley was concerned with something more universal, that tender connective tissue of *family* that came to him in the form of his grandmother's stories. Since the 1700s, they had been handed down dutifully across the generations, these memories of "The African" who hated his captivity so much that he tried four different times to escape; who had been seized from his native forest while chopping wood to make a drum, and when he tried to run away in America, his captors eventually cut off his foot. His new owner gave him the name of Toby, but he told the other slaves his name was "Kintay," and he pointed to the river that flowed nearby and uttered the words "Kamby Bolongo." All these things Alex Haley knew because his grandmother told him, and there were many times as a boy, and later as a man, when he tried to imagine this proud ancestor and the place he came from—his ebony blackness and the African forest—but was there really any way to *know?*

His determination to search for an answer crystallized at an unexpected moment. He was on a magazine assignment in London, having just finished writing *The Autobiography of Malcolm X*, a book that brought him his first taste of fame. He had spent a year interviewing the black nationalist leader and another year writing in Malcolm's words—a subtle and delicate journalistic assignment that in the end produced a book of high drama. With remarkable candor Malcolm related, and Haley shaped, the story of one black leader's evolution from street hustler to ascetic Black Muslim and eventually to a radical belief, despite his earlier professions to the contrary, in the possibility of racial reconciliation.

As Malcolm had predicted, he did not live to see the book published. On February 21, 1965, he was assassinated in Harlem, gunned down by followers of Elijah Muhammad, the Black Muslim leader with whom he had broken. Haley was distraught. He had come to regard Malcolm X as a friend, but in the end he knew there was nothing to do but move on. On his trip to London, he deliberately immersed himself in history, another time, another place, and on one of his stops at the British Museum, he found himself staring at the Rosetta Stone. Before that moment he had known of its existence, but only vaguely, and now here it was, a flat piece of rock from the Nile River Delta with three separate texts chiseled on its face. One text was in Greek, another in an unknown tongue, and the third in ancient hieroglyphics. Haley learned that a French scholar named Jean Champollion had successfully correlated the texts, beginning with the Greek—the *known*—and matching it character by character with the others.

On the plane ride back to the United States, Haley began to wonder if he, too, might be able to begin with the known—the sounds and the stories handed down across the years—and locate the origins of his family. For so many African Americans, he knew, the link to the past had been wiped out; really it was true for other people as well, but the Rosetta Stone analogy intrigued him. Could he begin with the family's oral history, bits and pieces of the past so lovingly preserved, and discover something new?

The idea soon became an obsession. He found a linguist at the University of Wisconsin who told him that the snippets of his ancestor's language appeared to be from the Mandinka tongue. The word "bolongo," he said, meant river; and "Kamby Bolongo," might well mean the Gambia River which flowed through an area where the language was spoken. Soon afterward, on a speaking trip to New York, Haley met Ebou Manga, a young college student who came from The Gambia, a West African country that took its name from the river. Manga became so intrigued by Haley's quest that he offered to go with him to The Gambia and see what the two of them could find.

On that trip Haley discovered that his African ancestor's name, Kintay—traditionally and properly spelled Kinte—belonged to a prominent family in The Gambia, and Haley soon found himself on a boat, headed upstream on the Gambia River to speak with one of the village *griots*. These were tribal elders trained in the art of memory, entrusted with the task of keeping the tribal history alive, of preserving old knowledge in the hearts of the living. When Haley came at last to the village of Jaffure, this was his description in *Roots* of his quite remarkable encounter with the *griot:*

The old man sat down, facing me, as the people hurriedly gathered behind him. Then he began to recite for me the ancestral history of the Kinte clan, as it had been passed along orally down across the centuries from the forefathers' time. It was not merely conversational, but more as if a scroll were being read; for the still, silent villagers, it was clearly a formal occasion.

For nearly two hours the *griot* spoke, adding a particular detail here or there, some fact about a person being named, until at last he came to Omoro Kinte, who had four sons. "About the time the King's soldiers came," the *griot* declared, "the oldest of these four sons, Kunta, went away from his village to chop wood . . . and he was never seen again." Haley was stunned, for he knew that according to his grand-mother's stories, their ancestor had been seized—carried away into slavery—while he was chopping wood to make a drum. Could this really be the same man? Despite the tantalizing power of the moment

Haley knew he was still operating in the realm of oral history, and his western mind wanted further proof.

He soon made another visit to London, and after two weeks of needle-in-the-haystack research, he discovered that in 1767 a British military unit had been sent from London to guard a slave fort on the Gambia River. Could this be when "the King's soldiers came"? Seven more weeks of poring through musty maritime records, and Haley discovered that on July 5, 1767, a British slave ship called *Lord Ligonier* had sailed from The Gambia to Annapolis, Maryland, the port to which his ancestor had come. He knew that much from his grandmother's stories. She had also told him that after the African's fourth attempt at escape, when the slave hunters had cut off his foot, he became the property of Dr. William Waller, who named him Toby. In Richmond, Virginia, Haley found the deed, a fraying paper dated September 5, 1768, giving Waller title to "one Negro man slave named Toby."

"My God!" Haley wrote in *Roots*. At last his journey of discovery was over. He still had a whole book to write, of course, but now he was sure that all of the old stories were true. He continued his study of the more general history, the dismal realities of the slave trade and of slavery itself, and through it all he developed a kind of composite understanding of his ancestor, Kunta Kinte. Part of it was what he *knew* to be true, and the rest of it was what he imagined; a literary form that some critics called *faction*. Some have criticized Haley for that, for a book in which the reader is left uncertain about what is really true and what isn't. There have also been professional genealogists who questioned his research, and an author who accused him of plagiarism, but despite the taint of those accusations the power of Haley's work—for me, at least—is still undeniable. Following its publication in 1976, *Roots* won a Pulitzer Prize and a National Book

Award, and the following year the *Roots* miniseries won an Emmy.

And for people lucky enough to know him, there was the direct inspiration of Haley himself. I met him only once, in 1988, but even today one of my prized literary possessions is a copy of *Roots* inscribed quite warmly to my wife and me: "To Frye and Nancy—Love! Alex Haley." The occasion on which I acquired that inscription was a banquet in honor of a mutual friend, Dr. C. Eric Lincoln, one of the great black scholars of the twentieth century. Both Haley and Lincoln had written extensively about Malcolm X and had developed a bond of mutual admiration. In 1988, as Lincoln was completing a fine Southern novel called *The Avenue, Clayton City*, Haley read the manuscript for him and sent him a cryptic note of affirmation: "C. Eric, you can write your ass off! Ain't nothing wrong with this manuscript except that you wrote it instead of me."

As it happened, I was writing a profile of Lincoln not long after that letter arrived, and we talked at length about *The Avenue, Clayton City*, and about Alex Haley, and about Dr. Lincoln's north Alabama boyhood that had deeply influenced his writing and his life. He had come of age in the cotton country near the town of Athens, raised by his grandparents, Less and Mattie Lincoln, who had taught him to "respect everybody respectable." That included whites as well as blacks, and many of the whites Lincoln knew growing up tended to treat him decently enough. But there was one exception. On a late Autumn day, probably in 1937 when Lincoln was a boy of thirteen, he carried a forty-pound bag of cotton to the local gin. He was proud of the fact that at nine cents a pound that would mean $3.60 for his family, and he was startled, therefore, when the cotton gin owner—a white man—casually flipped him a quarter.

"Mr. Beasley," Eric said softly, "I think you made a mistake."

Beasley's face turned red and he got up abruptly and bolted the door. At first the boy was merely puzzled, but he suddenly found himself sprawled on the floor, gasping for breath from a blow to his midsection, as Beasley began to kick him and stomp on his head. "He was in a frenzy," Lincoln remembered, "and I'll never forget his words: 'Nigger, as long as you live, don't you *never* try to count behind no white man again."

As Lincoln told the story in 1988, his large, dark eyes welled over with tears, and for both of us, I think, it was an unexpected moment of intimacy that cemented a friendship lasting until Lincoln's death. Later that year when he won the Lillian Smith Award for Southern fiction, he asked me to come to the awards banquet and to share the head table with Alex Haley, who was there to make a talk in his honor. Awed of course by the august company, I was soon put at ease by Haley's amiability and warmth, and by what seemed to be his genuine interest in what I was writing. I told him a little about my grandfather's stories and about the cardboard box I had found in his attic—that dusty collection of old family letters—and I told him also about Robert Croshon, who had worked for my family for more than sixty years. Robert was a gardener, an African American man of gentle dignity, who was also a fine storyteller. He told his own family, and later told me, about Gilbert Fields, his great-grandfather, who was born in Africa and later enslaved. Apparently a proud and restless man, Fields fled from his Georgia plantation one night with his wife, two daughters, and a granddaughter. They intended to follow the Big Dipper north, but a sudden thunderstorm came up, blotting out the stars, and in the confusion that followed the family headed south. They came to a cave near the Alabama line where another runaway was living underground. He took them in, told them they could stay, but they headed south instead to Mobile, where they quietly entered its community of free Negroes.

I told all this to Alex Haley, who firmly replied: "You have to write that." And so I did.

II

When I think about the legacy of Alex Haley and his odyssey in search of his roots, my mind often jumps to the work of Rick Bragg—one of the most gifted nonfiction writers in the South. Bragg is a former newspaper man who honed his craft to a Pulitzer Prize-winning edge before setting off to write best sellers. He is known today for a fiercely affectionate trilogy about his family—one book about his mother, another about fatherhood, and in between there was *Ava's Man*, the story of his grandfather, Charlie Bundrum, a hard-living son of the Southern foothills, renowned in the family for his great and tender heart. Bundrum died a year before his grandson was born ("I've never forgiven him for that," Bragg wrote), and in trying to reconstruct the pieces of his life, Bragg, like a lot of us, thought about Haley.

"*Roots* was an eye-opening book for me and for a lot of Southerners," he said. "If it were not for oral histories there would have been no books from me at all. I sat for days and days and just listened to my people talk, about killings and shootings and stabbings and fistfights, and about running off to get married, or just running off, and about jail, and bad police, and commodity cheese, and drunks, and all of it. I learned how they felt about each other, what they feared, and what they dreamed about."

Bragg set out to write it down, a different dimension of the great Southern story—the memories of white people who grew up poor and often stayed that way; people who loved to tell a good story, but until fairly recently wouldn't put it to paper. Maybe they didn't know how to write, or maybe they had other things on their minds, like scratching out a living from the soil or the mills, or maybe they just thought the stories were enough. But sometime around the middle of the twentieth century, a new generation came along, writers as passionate as any I've read. There was Tim McLaurin from North Carolina, an alcoholic former Peace Corps volunteer and Marine Corps veteran who loved to get drunk and pick up snakes, and who wrote a novel called *Cured by Fire*—the tragic story of two homeless men, one white, one black, who form a friendship across the divide. And there was also Harry Crews, a white sharecropper's son from southern Georgia, whose novels are full of crazy people and freaks, and who also wrote a haunting memoir about his own growing up, *A Childhood: The Biography of a Place*. This is how Crews began that story:

My first memory is of a time ten years before I was born, and the memory takes place where I have never been and involves my daddy whom I never knew. It was the middle of the night in the Everglades swamp in 1925, when my daddy woke his best friend Cecil out of a deep sleep in the bunkhouse just south of the floating dredge that was slowly chewing its way across the Florida Peninsula . . . The night was dark as only a swamp can be dark and they could not see each other there in the bunkhouse. The rhythmic stroke of the dredge's engine came counterpoint to my daddy's shaky voice as he told Cecil what was wrong.

When Cecil finally did speak, he said: "I hope it was good, boy. I sho do."
"What was good?"
"That Indian. You got the clap."

Such is the literary tradition out of which Bragg came by way of a stop at the *New York Times*. That was where I first encountered his work, and I'll never forget his lead on a story about the Oklahoma City bombing. He was part of the team of *Times* reporters sent to

Oklahoma on April 19, 1995, after a fanatic by the name of Timothy McVeigh filled a Ryder truck with five thousand pounds of fertilizer—ammonium nitrate—and lit the fuse. The explosion killed one hundred and sixty-eight people, including children at a daycare center, and what can anyone say in such a moment? Can a reporter really find the words? Maybe not, but this is how Bragg wrote it:

> *Before the dust and the rage had a chance to settle, a chilly rain started to fall on the blasted-out wreck of what had once been an office building, and on the shoulders of the small army of police, firefighters and medical technicians that surrounded it. They were not used to this, if anyone is. On any other day, they would have answered calls to kitchen fires, domestic disputes, or even a cat up a tree . . . "We're just a little old cowtown," said Bill Finn, a grime-covered firefighter who propped himself wearily against a brick wall as the rain turned the dust to mud on his face. "You can't get no more Middle America than Oklahoma City . . ."*

As the *Times* coverage continued to unfold, I thought it was literature on deadline, for it's always been a role of good writing to turn tragedy into something akin to beauty, and thus make it bearable. But it was also clear that in Bragg's accounts were the obvious seeds of a larger possibility—of stretching out as a writer and telling a story that would fill up a book. And sure enough, the first one came in 1999. He called it *All Over but the Shoutin'* and it was a story about his mama. What Bragg delivered his first time out was a portrait of suffering, love, and sacrifice, and he did it in the style of a fine feature writer, writing with emotion that he wore on his sleeve, but sensing deftly when to rein it in.

"*All Over but the Shoutin'* is a work of art," wrote Pat Conroy after reading the book. "I never met Rick Bragg in my life, but I called him up and told him he'd written a masterpiece, and I sent flowers to his mother."

Such effusive praise was not at all uncommon, and Bragg was suddenly a literary star. But what exactly could he do for an encore? The answer turned out to be *Ava's Man*, a book I thought was equally impressive, for Bragg this time was writing about a person he never knew, piecing together his grandfather's character from family recollections, some of which were offered with reluctance. It was not, he discovered, that people felt the need to protect Charlie Bundrum, not that they were ashamed, but rather that more than forty years after his death, the memory of it was too much to bear. "After Daddy died," Rick's mother told him, "it was like there was nothing."

Charlie was born poor and died that way, but not for lack of back-breaking work. He grew to manhood with the Great Depression, which came early and stayed late in his particular corner of the South, and as Bragg makes clear in *Ava's Man*, it carried its own special brand of hurt.

> *It is true that almost everyone in the foothills farmed and hunted, so there were no breadlines, no men holding signs that begged for work and food, no children going door to door, as they did in Atlanta, asking for table scraps. Here, deep in the woods, was a different agony. Babies, the most tenuous, died from poor diet and simple things, like fevers and dehydration. In Georgia, one in seven babies died before their first birthday, and in Alabama it was worse.*

Charlie Bundrum lost one baby, but he scrapped and fought and he and Ava raised seven others, and mostly they grew up happy and strong. But they also learned that life was hard and a little bit mean, and a lot of the time you had to keep moving to stay ahead of trouble. That's what Charlie and the rest of them did, moving more than twenty times, back and forth across the Georgia line, swapping one rented house for another, most of them hidden way back in the woods. In places such as these, Charlie could fish and hunt and work for pay when the work was there, digging wells, putting roofs on houses, and to supplement the family income he could also make a little moonshine. He loved to sample his own wares and many a night his wise and patient horse named Bob would have to find the way home and deposit Charlie gently in the front yard. But Charlie never got mean when he drank, never loved his family any less, and that love was the thing that everyone remembered. It could turn suddenly fierce if his children were threatened, but most of the time it was tender and generous and extended to neighbors down on their luck. He even brought home a hermit one time, a gnome-like man who lived in a shack hidden down by the river, and Charlie just made him part of the family, became his protector, to save him from the bullies who nearly beat him to death. And so, writes Bragg, even four decades after his death the memories of Charlie were strong and bittersweet.

I remember the night, an icy night in December, I asked three of Charlie Bundrum's daughters to tell me about his funeral. I sat in embarrassment as my aunts, all in their sixties, just stared hard at the floor. Juanita, tough as whalebone and hell, began to softly cry, and Jo, who has survived Uncle John and ulcers, wiped at her eyes. My mother, Margaret, got up and left the room. For coffee, she said.

I admit to being a sucker for these family stories, for all of Bragg's books, and for memoirs like the late Tim Russert's *Big Russ and Me* or Calvin Trillin's *Messages from My Father*. And even in the world of fiction a writer like Winston Groom in *Forrest Gump*—amid all the irony, humor, and satire—could add in layers of meaning and heart by the story of a mother's love for her son. But there is, of course, another dimension to this complicated subject. From William Shakespeare to William Faulkner, Zora Neale Hurston to Alice Walker, writers have probed the dark, fertile ground of family dysfunction, that corner of life in which people feel most free to be who they are. As many of us know, there are times when this is not a good thing—which brings us inevitably to Pat Conroy.

III

Before I read *The Great Santini*, and thus considered the depths of Conroy's rage, I had read his first best seller, *The Water Is Wide*. I found it delightful. Here was a memoir, with a few name changes to protect the innocent, of a young teacher's time on Daufuskie Island, South Carolina, a place of stark and moss-draped beauty, where a small population of African Americans—still speaking, in fact, in the dialects of Africa, still traveling by ox cart on the island's sandy roads—lived as if the mainland were a thousand miles away, instead of just three. And this was 1969.

It is true, looking back, that there were hints of Conroy's molten anger hidden in the pages of *The Water Is Wide*, though at the time it seemed like moral indignation. He had come, after all, to a wooden schoolhouse where the children had been so neglected through the years that they didn't know which country they were living in, which ocean washed upon the shores of their island, or who was president of the United States. Their best guess was John Kennedy, for they had heard that he was good to black people, and they reasoned that if he were the current and the greatest of all presidents, he was probably also the first. They had never heard of George Washington.

"Sweet little Jesus," Conroy thought, gazing at their faces on the first day of class, "these kids don't know crap."

Not knowing precisely where to begin, he launched a scattergun assault on a wasteland of ignorance, regaling his fifth- through eighth-graders with stories of the greatest classical composers while he played their music on a crude phonograph; or forcing the class to listen every morning to the radio news, while he pointed out the global hotspots on the map—Vietnam, Israel, the nations of Europe—and he did it all with a needling sense of humor that came to him naturally. As the year progressed, the students grew to love him, and he took delight when official visitors made their way to the island, primed most often for condescension or pity, in putting his students through their paces, identifying the music of Beethoven or Brahms.

But in the end the authorities were not amused. On his third day on the job, Conroy wrote a blistering letter to the superintendent of schools, decrying the official neglect of Daufuskie, and though he obviously spoke the truth, his diplomatic skills could have used a little work. After a year of righteous proclamations he was fired, and when *The Water Is Wide* came out in 1972, I read it first as a political protest, an expose of racism in a quaint, forgotten corner of the South. It was only when I read *The Great Santini* that I began to understand—like a lot of other readers, I suppose—the reason for Conroy's problem with authority, especially when the power was abused or misused.

Santini tells the story of a Marine fighter pilot by the name of Bull Meacham, who is bombastic, overbearing, and sometimes violent toward the members of his family. He has some other qualities also, giving the story its subtlety and depth. He is a fearless warrior and defender of his country, a skillful pilot and leader of men, and it is clear that he loves his wife and four children, and they love him. But they live their lives in an undertow of dread, tiptoeing through the dangers of Bull Meacham's moods, and their caution ultimately is never enough. Meacham's tyranny and explosions of fury eventually, inevitably turn to abuse, and the target most often is his oldest son, Ben.

Ben is a boy with the soul of a poet. He is a star on the high school basketball team, and he possesses a kind of dogged self-esteem even in the face of his father's tirades. But he also suffers along with the other members of his family. Once just before he turns eighteen, he and his father are locked in a game of one-on-one at the basketball court in the family driveway. In Ben's whole life, not one of the Meacham children has ever beaten their father at anything—not even checkers, but on this occasion Ben is too quick for the Great Santini, the name Bull Meacham has given himself, ostensibly as a joke. But winning and losing are not a joking matter, and when Ben wins the game by a single point, the Great Santini explodes in a rage.

Bull took the basketball and threw it into Ben's forehead. Ben turned to walk into the house, but Bull followed him, matching his steps and throwing the basketball against his son's head at intervals of three steps. Bull kept chanting, "Cry, cry, cry," each time the ball ricocheted off his son's skull. Through the kitchen Ben marched, through the dining room, never putting his hands behind his head to protect himself, never trying to dodge the ball. Ben just walked and with all his powers of concentration . . . tried not to cry. That was all he wanted to derive from the experience, the knowledge that he had not cried.

As Conroy's career continued to unfold, evolving through novels like *The Prince of Tides* and later *Beach Music*, he employed the agony of family dysfunction to explore the darkness of the human condition. These were, I thought, magnificent, disturbing works of art, with language that reminded me of Lillian Smith or Robert Penn Warren, those most poetic of all Southern writers. And if any of us wondered how much of it was true, how much was rooted in the literal experience of his own family, Conroy would later offer up an answer. In 1999, he wrote an article for *Atlanta* magazine called "The Death of Santini," telling the story of his Marine Corps father, Donald Conroy, who died in 1998. In this quite startling piece, this is a part of what Conroy wrote:

I did not tell the whole truth in The Great Santini *by any means. I lacked the courage and I thought that if I told the truth about Donald Conroy that no one would believe me and that no one would want to read a book that contained so much unprovoked humiliation and violence. It was not just that my father was mean, his meanness seemed grotesque and exaggerated and overblown to me . . . I can barely look back on my sorrowful youth, yet it haunts my every waking moment and makes me a terrible husband, father and friend. My childhood rides with me and I cannot shake it off or dull its murderous power over me. I always thought that the sight of my father's corpse would be one of the happiest days of my life. I thought I would be fawn-like and boyish as I danced on his grave and urinated on his headstone . . .*

And yet there was also redemption in the story, remarkable given the severity of the wounds, and it all began with *The Great Santini.* When Donald Conroy read the book he was furious. He brooded and grieved at his son's betrayal, at what he insisted was a cruel and distorted portrait of himself, but slowly and resolutely over time he also did something else. Incredibly, according to Pat Conroy, the real Santini willed a new identity for himself, displayed a kind of strength and courage more subtle and profound—more reflective of the ultimate power of *family*—than the courage he had shown on the battlefields of war.

He returned to his children in the disguise of The Great Santini—*the fictional one, not the real one. He became the Santini who gave his son Ben a flight jacket on his eighteenth birthday, the one who sent his daughter Mary Anne flowers at her first prom, who left his duty as an Officer of the Guard when his son got in trouble . . . By an act of sheer stubbornness and will, my father used my first novel to transform himself into something resembling a most wonderful man.*

These are the most surprising words I have ever written.

They are also some of the most surprising that I have ever read, the poetry of hurt, and the poetry of love, from a writer who has demonstrated over time an inexhaustible understanding of each.

· 10 ·

The Classics and the Glory of the Stars

FEATURING:

Ahab's Wife—Sena Jeter Naslund

Year of Wonders—Geraldine Brooks

Adam & Eve—Sena Jeter Naslund

ALSO, HERMAN MELVILLE, WILLIAM SHAKESPEARE,
LAURA INGALLS WILDER, NATHANIEL HAWTHORNE,
PETER BENCHLEY, THOMAS HARDY

I

IT WAS A book that literally began with a vision. One clear spring night in 1993, Sena Jeter Naslund was driving a rented car through Boston when an image suddenly sprang from her mind, almost as if she could see it with her eyes. There was a woman standing on a widow's walk, gazing out across the harbor, waiting for her husband's ship to come home. Suddenly, the woman is struck full-force with the knowledge that the ship is not coming—not that night, and in fact, not ever—for something terrible has happened at sea. And before the grief can sweep her away, she finds herself staring at the star-filled sky, asking the most basic question of all: *Who am I in the face of this vast glory? What's my place in the universe?*

This celestial image that came unbidden was not the only inspiration for *Ahab's Wife*, a novel of soaring ambition and beauty that is surely one of the finest of our time. There was also a journey that Sena Naslund made with her daughter, just the two of them traveling by car, listening mile after mile to books on tape. As Naslund recounted the trip years later, her daughter Flora was then eleven, and Sena wanted to share with her the books that she had loved as a girl. She had, in fact, been quite a bookworm as a child growing up in Birmingham, Alabama. One of her earliest reading memories was of a hot summer day when she was maybe ten and reading a Laura Ingalls Wilder book, so caught in a passage about a blizzard on the prairie that she suddenly realized she was cold.

"It was over ninety degrees," Naslund remembered, "but these words I was reading had made me shiver. I said to myself, 'I'd like to be able to do that someday.'"

And so her passion for the written word grew. She read *Little Women*, reveling in the tomboy world of Jo March, and then *Moby Dick* when she was thirteen, followed by *Jane Eyre*, *War and Peace*, and most of Charles Dickens. During high school, she began to develop her love of Shakespeare, reading *Macbeth* and *Hamlet*, and on an English paper about *Julius Caesar* she received a grade of A++++.

She began to think harder about being a writer.

Many years later, Sena wanted her daughter to understand such things—the power and the passion of a well-written story—and as she and Flora began their summer of travel, she picked the books they would listen to together. There was *Little Women*, of course, and

Adventures of Huckleberry Finn, and most significantly, as it turned out, there was *Moby Dick.* Naslund was surprised that this was Flora's favorite, for it was not simply the adventure or the terrible menace of the Great White Whale that seemed to leave the little girl entranced, but the roll of Herman Melville's language.

> *I have fed upon dry salted fare—fit emblem of the day nourishment of my soul!—when the poorest landsman has had fresh fruit to his daily hand, and broken the world's fresh bread to my mouldy crusts—away, whole oceans away, from that young girl-wife I wedded past fifty, and sailed for Cape Horn the next day, leaving but one dent in my marriage pillow—wife? wife?—rather a widow with her husband alive! Aye, I widowed that poor girl when I married her . . . and then, the madness, the frenzy, the boiling blood and the smoking brow, with which, for a thousand lowerings old Ahab has furiously, foamingly chased his prey—more a demon than a man!*

Sena shared her daughter's fascination with the words, but sadly this time, for it occurred to her that in this grand and glorious story, this Shakespearean mixture of tragedy and quest, there was not a strong woman character to be found. Melville, she noticed, had not even named the wife of Ahab, the whaling captain possessed by hatred of the whale Moby Dick, and in that failing—and in the shining eyes of her daughter—Naslund saw an opportunity for herself. She wanted to create a female character, complicated, strong and deeply sympathetic, who could take her place beside Hester Prynne in the great pantheon of American letters. Naslund admired Nathaniel Hawthorne's Prynne, the persecuted heroine in *The Scarlet Letter*—a Puritan woman who, thinking that her husband is dead, conceives a child out of wedlock and resolutely refuses to identify the father. Though scorned by her community and forced to wear the scarlet letter *A* as a symbol of adultery, Prynne ultimately emerges in the course of the novel as a woman secure in her own identity.

As John Updike would later write, "She is a mythic version of every woman's attempt to integrate her sexuality with societal demands."

But Naslund knew there was something else about Hester Prynne that made her the object of enduring fascination. With the possible exception of Scarlet O'Hara she had stood nearly alone in American fiction as a strong and memorable female character, a hero to compare with Captain Ahab or Huckleberry Finn, Willie Stark, Tom Joad, or Atticus Finch. And so it was that on a clear spring night in 1993, driving her rental car through Boston, Sena saw a young woman on a widow's walk, scanning the harbor for her seafaring husband, and thinking these words: *Captain Ahab was neither my first husband nor my last.*

She knew she had the first sentence of her novel.

She would travel once again the path that Herman Melville had chosen, but with a woman character this time, a woman whose strength would be a mirror and a match for the character of Captain Ahab. Naslund, in fact, thought she saw possibilities for developing a side of Ahab that Melville had hinted at, but left unfinished. Remembered mostly for his raging fury, his obsession with revenge against the whale who had earlier cost him a leg, the great sea captain, Naslund believed, had been a man of sensitivity and intellect. She plumbed the depths of *Moby Dick*, searching for evidence to support this view, and among other things, found the testimonial of a fellow sea captain:

Ahab's above the common; Ahab's been in colleges, as well as 'mong the cannibals; been used to deeper wonders than the waves; fixed his fiery lance in mightier, stranger foes than whales . . . Ahab has his humanities!

It was a measure of the audacity of *Ahab's Wife* that Sena Naslund set out not to alter, but to enlarge one of the largest characters in American fiction. And having done that, she made him a *secondary* character in her novel, for it is certainly true that the strongest character in *Ahab's Wife* is not Ahab, but Una, once an innocent farm girl from Kentucky, who as part of her odyssey of spirit and flesh, marries Ahab and bears him a child. Before that happens Una has already been to sea, a stowaway on a whaling vessel in love with two young members of the crew.

As part of the model for Una's voyage, Naslund relied upon a book by Owen Chase, who had been first mate on the whale ship *Essex*. On August 12, 1819, the *Essex* sailed from Nantucket harbor, but the following year a sperm whale turned on the ship and rammed it twice, sending the shattered vessel to the bottom. Twenty-one men initially survived, scrambling into three open boats, but because of a terrible miscalculation only eight were rescued. Owen Chase was one of the eight, and his account of the voyage, *Narrative of the Most Extraordinary and Distressing Shipwreck of the Whale-Ship Essex*, was said to be Herman Melville's inspiration for *Moby Dick*.

When Sena Naslund read Chase's book she was startled by the irony at the heart of the story. The *Essex* survivors stood a good chance of drifting to the Marquesas Islands, some twelve hundred miles to the west. That was the plan of Captain George Pollard, but the mutinous crew, led by Chase, feared there were cannibals living on the islands and demanded instead that they aim for South America. It was a fatal mistake, a voyage of more than four thousand miles, skirting the trade winds blowing from the east, and before they could make it they ran out of food. Desperate, the crew drew lots to see which of their number would be sacrificed so that the other survivors might eat. The loser was the cabin boy, who was said to declare: "It is as good a fate as any."

In *Ahab's Wife* Naslund put her young protagonist Una in that same bloody boat, one of three survivors in her tale. The other two are Giles and Kit, the two young men whom Una has loved, unable to decide which of them to marry. They are compelled as friends to live with the terrible memory of their deed, their descent into cannibalism to survive. The burden proves too much for the men, one of whom dies, the other of whom is driven into madness, beyond the ability of Una to reach him. But Una moves on, and in the course of this rich and satisfying story—this most majestic of American novels—she finds not only solace, but spiritual redemption. Part of it comes in her marriage to Ahab, the captain who helped to rescue her at sea. She is surprised at first that this would be so, for he is a man much older than she. But she finds him tender and passionate and wise, and she grieves for his wounds at the jaws of Moby Dick; grieves for his physical torment and pain, and grieves also for his obsession with revenge.

Finally, of course, she grieves for his death, but even then she will not give in to the lure of despair. She finds new meaning in the company of friends, who introduce her to perhaps the greatest moral cause of her time, the abolition of slavery, and to the burgeoning worlds of literature and science. Late in the book Una stands alone on a night in Nantucket and gazes up at the star-filled sky, asking the questions that haunt the human mind.

Where is my place before this swirling ball of star mass, edgeless and expansive, without horizon? Where is my place, when I know that this is but one of ten billion? Here the categories crack. Beauty—that gilt frame—burns at its edges and falls to ash. Love? It's no more than a blade of grass. Perhaps there is music *here, for in all that swirling perhaps harmony fixes the giants in their turning, marches them always outward in their fiery parade.*

II

As I was reading this novel for the first time, with all its grandeur and all its multiple layers of meaning, I thought of another book from the late twentieth century that owes a certain debt to *Moby Dick*. In Peter Benchley's *Jaws*, the villainous fish is not a whale, but a great white shark. But there is a character reminiscent of Ahab—a professional shark hunter named Quint, played in the movie by the great Robert Shaw, who develops his own Shakespearean obsession. (Who can forget the scene in the film where Quint, like Ahab, is killed by his prey?) But whatever its moments of literary pretension, it is clear from the start that the ultimate purpose of Benchley's work is page-turning terror, for it is, without apology or shame, a frankly commercial piece of good writing.

Ahab's Wife, of course, is not. But like *Jaws* it became a runaway best seller, and there is hope and inspiration in that. I can think of few other books which explore the human condition at greater depth, or offer more clearly the reassuring notion that we are part of something larger than ourselves. Naslund came naturally to such understandings. Certainly, in Birmingham, as a young adult in the civil rights years, she saw the ambiguity of the human heart, our ability to embrace both good and evil, and sometimes both at once. Like many of us in those years, Naslund vowed to write about what she had seen, particularly after the Birmingham church bombing, perhaps the most horrible tragedy of the time.

In 2003, she published *Four Spirits*, a civil rights novel both passionate and vast, but I remember wondering when I first heard about the book what a novelist could do with this subject matter that a historian with the right sensibilities could not. Diane McWhorter, another Birmingham writer, had just won a Pulitzer Prize for her historical memoir *Carry Me Home*, and as it happened I was completing a civil rights book of my own which was set for publication the following spring. I didn't begrudge Sena Naslund her novel; far from it, for I already knew and respected her work. Still, I wondered how any writer would manage to improve on the literal truth.

I had recently been to Birmingham and interviewed the Reverend John Cross, minister of the Sixteenth Street Baptist Church, the target of the Sunday morning bomb. It was a day, Cross said, that began with such promise: September 15, 1963, full of bright sunshine and the singing of birds, a morning when the older children in the church would serve as ushers and sing in the choir at the main Sunday service. But at 10:29 the bomb exploded. When Cross first felt the building shake, he thought momentarily of the water heater. They had been having trouble with it, and he wondered if the pipes had finally blown. But he heard people screaming and rushed outside and saw a gaping hole in the wall. He quickly joined those digging through the rubble and uncovered a patent leather shoe.

"That's Denise's shoe," said M. W. Pippin, a church layman who was frantically digging beside him. Pippin knew his granddaughter, Denise McNair, often wore the same kind of shoe, and almost as soon as he had spoken the words he and Cross came upon the bodies—first Denise and then her friends, Cynthia Wesley, Carole Robertson, and Addie Mae Collins. As tears of rage streamed down Pippin's face, he screamed aloud what many people felt: "I'd like to blow the whole town up."

Then came the most astonishing part. Three days later Martin Luther King Jr. preached the eulogy for the children, and this is what he said:

History has proven over and over again that unmerited suffering is redemptive. . . . So in spite of the darkness of this hour we must not despair. We must not become bitter, nor must we harbor the desire to retaliate with violence. We must not lose faith in our white brothers. Somehow we must believe that even the most misguided among them can learn to respect the dignity and worth of all human personalities.

I had always wondered how the sermon was received. How could the people in the church that day, including the shattered families of the children, possibly have listened to such noble words? On a magazine assignment a few years later, I came to Birmingham to interview Claude Wesley, father of Cynthia. Mr. Wesley was a principal in the Birmingham schools, a thin and wispy, gray-haired man who wanted his students to understand black history, the taproots of freedom going back a hundred years. We took our seats in his living room, and he explained that he saw the bombing that way, as a terrible, heartbreaking, personal loss that was nevertheless part of a much bigger story. As he talked, he glanced at a portrait on the wall, a radiant smile on the round, pretty face.

"Such a beautiful girl," I said.

"Yes," he replied, "she was a very happy child. She always liked to be in the forefront. Her teachers used to say if they could get Cynthia on their side, they could get the whole class."

We talked for a while about the Birmingham movement and the changes he had seen in the city. "Birmingham is now a good town," he said. "It wanted to be a good town then, but there were some forces standing in the way."

Finally, I came to the question I had driven all the way to Birmingham to ask. What about the eulogy? How did it feel to be called to forgiveness when bitterness and rage were the natural inclinations?

Wesley's answer was quick and emphatic. "We never felt bitter," he said. "That would not have been fair to Cynthia. We try to deal with her memory the same way we dealt with her presence, and bitterness had no place in that. And there was something else we never did. We never said, 'Why us?' because that would be the same thing as asking, 'Why not somebody else?'"

When I heard Claude Wesley speak those words I thought I had never encountered a faith so profound, a Christian understanding that ran any deeper, and it offered such a startling contrast to the hideous act that put it to the test. The bomb that exploded in 1963 may have blown the face of Jesus from the stained-glass window on the side of the church. But the hearts of the faithful had survived the wound, and in their survival had offered a redemption such as our country had rarely ever seen. So, at least, it seemed to me and how could a novelist improve on that?

The answer, of course, was much simpler than the question. Sena Naslund came at the movement indirectly. In her novel, *Four Spirits*, she wrote with the fundamental understanding that even as history was being made—and of course everybody knew that it was—the people of Birmingham, particularly the white people, continued to pursue their daily lives, mundane in the shadow of the civil rights story. Among her many other advantages, a novelist can grasp the irony of that fact far better than a journalist or a historian, without losing touch with the larger truth.

I thought Naslund succeeded superbly, and after I finished reading *Four Spirits* I moved on to her other books. One was *Abundance*, a novel about Marie Antoinette, the frequently vilified Queen of France whom many remember for saying, "Let them eat cake." Naslund rediscovered that story on a trip to Georgia. She found a book in the bed-and-breakfast lobby, a biography of Marie published in 1932 by Austrian writer Stefan Zweig. Naslund was offended by the book.

"The Zweig biography suggested that Marie Antoinette led a compelling and exciting life," she recalled, "but I felt he treated her in an unfair and condescending manner. The subtitle of the biography was *The Portrait of an Average Woman*, and it was clear that Zweig considered the average woman to be none too bright, selfish and egotistical, materialistic and extravagant."

With her feminist juices stirred, as well as her sense of elemental fairness, Naslund began to study the contemporary scholarship on Marie. Already, she was fascinated by the history—the violent days of the French Revolution when the notion of democracy ran amok and ultimately led, among other things, to the beheading of both the King and the Queen. On multiple occasions, Sena had read Charles Dickens's *A Tale of Two Cities*, such a vivid evocation of the times, and as she learned more and more about Marie she decided to write her story as a novel.

Naslund discovered in the course of her research that Marie had never said, "Let them eat cake." On the contrary, this woman who became a queen as a girl—the daughter of royalty born to that realm—felt a sense of compassion for the poor, as did her husband, King Louis XVI. But as the French Revolution spun out of control, the King and the Queen became the scapegoats of a national desperation, giving their story, as Naslund understood it, the elements of a Shakespearean tragedy. She structured her novel in precisely that way—five acts leading to a deadly conclusion, but with a touch of redemption at the end. Even the most critical biographers agree that Marie Antoinette faced death on the newly invented guillotine with extraordinary courage. Thus, Naslund ended her story this way:

All my body feels full of air. I seem to weigh nothing, and I move with great ease, almost as though I were dancing. I step down the little stair placed at the end of the cart. My balance is sure, and I forget that my hands are bound. I do not need them. Weightless, I mount the scaffold stairs. But on the platform, I tread upon a fleshy lump. I have stepped on the toe of Sanson, the executioner. Quickly, I beg pardon.

"I did not do it on purpose," I say with simple sincerity.

As I savored the grace of this extraordinary novel, only one other writer came to mind—only one author in the twenty-first century who aims as high or finds her stories in a similar way. Like Sena Naslund, Geraldine Brooks has plumbed the depths of classic literature and history to find a meaning for our time. In 2005 she won a Pulitzer Prize for her novel, *March*, in which she developed the character of "Mr. March," the absent father in *Little Women*.

My favorite among Brooks's novels is *Year of Wonders*, a remarkable story set in 1666. The heart of it is literally true. In that year, the bubonic plague descended on the English village of Eyam, where the residents made a remarkable choice. They decided not to flee the disease, but to quarantine themselves, thus preventing a spread to other towns. They were guided in that extraordinary act by a young and charismatic minister named William Montpesson, who lost his own wife to the ravage of the plague.

All of this was a matter of history—a story that Geraldine Brooks discovered while she was living in London, covering the world's trouble spots for the *Wall Street Journal*. Interspersed among her trips to Gaza, Somalia, Bosnia, or Baghdad, she often made jaunts to the English countryside, seeking rest and renewal in those rugged mountains. In the summer of 1990, on a recreational visit to Derbyshire, she came upon a roadside sign pointing the way to the PLAGUE VILLAGE. Transfixed by the history, she vowed to write about it some day, choosing as a form the historical novel.

Her narrator is a woman she calls Anna Frith, a maid to the village minister and his family. Anna is a young and attractive widow, a mother of two, in this Puritanical lead-mining town. In the spring that follows her husband's death she takes in a boarder, George Viccars, a journeyman tailor, who slowly but surely becomes her suitor. *I thought God had sent him. Later, there were those who would say it had been the devil.* Before their love can be consummated, Viccars is stricken by the bubonic plague, having been the one to introduce it to the village. In a matter of hours, his fever surges and his body is covered with boils and sores—those horrible symptoms that, in later centuries, physicians would discover are necrotic lymph nodes.

As Viccars dies and the epidemic spreads, the village minister preaches to the people. (The author has called him Michael Montpellion, a name that connotes his similarity to William Montpesson, the actual figure in history, but leaves maneuvering room for fiction.) As Brooks understands him, the minister is idealistic and strong, a man of courage and a man of faith as he looks from the pulpit of his church and declares:

Beloved, I hear you in your hearts, saying that we already fear. We fear this disease and the death it brings. But you will not leave this fear behind you. It will travel with you wheresoever you fly. And on your way, it will gather to itself a host of greater fears. For if you sicken in a stranger's house, they may turn you out, they may abandon you, they may lock you up to die in dreadful solitude. You will thirst, and none shall quench you. You will cry out, and your cries will fade into empty air. For in that stranger's house, all you will receive is blame. For surely they will blame you, for bringing this thing to them. And they will blame you justly! And they will heap their hatred upon you, in the hour when your greatest need is love.

In the village of Eyam, the people are deeply moved by the words, but in the end the suffering is simply too much. More than two-thirds of the villagers die, and among the survivors the terror mutates from a fear of sickness to a fear of each other. Even the young minister, before it is through, is dragged from his faith to the depths of despair. Only Anna is left unshattered, able to cling, if not to her faith then at least to her hope.

In fashioning such a strong central character, Brooks draws on some of her work as a journalist, remembering the women she has met in other places:

Anna's character and the changes it undergoes were suggested to me by the lives of women I had met during my years as a reporter in the Middle East and Africa—women who had lived lives that were highly circumscribed and restricted, until thrown into sudden turmoil by a crisis such as war or famine . . . I saw women who had traveled enormous personal distances— traditional village women in Eritrea who became platoon leaders in the country's independence war; Kurdish women who led their families to safety over mined mountain passes after the failure of their uprising against Saddam Hussein. If those women could change and grow so remarkably, I reasoned that Anna could, too.

But there was another, more disturbing similarity between the time Brooks was writing about in her novel and the time she has written about as a journalist. *Year of Wonders* appeared in 2001, the year of the 9-11 attacks, and she was struck by the initial acts of heroism—the firefighters rushing up the steps of the towers, the passengers on United Flight 93—and how all of that, as well as our national sense of unity, slowly, inexorably gave way to our fear.

One thing I believe completely is that the human heart remains the human heart, no matter how our material circumstances change as we move together through time.

III

As I finished reading *Year of Wonders* it occurred to me that it may well be—perhaps along with *Ahab's Wife*—one of the first classics of the twenty-first century. Certainly, the artistry and ambition are there, for these two novelists, it seems to me, are aiming as high and reaching as deep as any I've read. Nor are they finished. In Sena Naslund's most recent novel, *Adam & Eve*, published in 2010, she lifts her gaze from the human heart to the immensity of creation itself. She always loved *The Return of the Native*, Thomas Hardy's novel that opened with a scene on the British heath. The people are lighting bonfires in the night—"little lights answering the lights in the vastness," as Naslund put it. It made her think of a contemporary poem, one she used as an epigraph for *Ahab's Wife*.

One must take off her fear like clothing;
One must travel at night;
This is the seeking after God.

Those words written by Maureen Morehead are, in a sense, the philosophical framework for *Adam & Eve*, a book that begins where *Ahab* ended—not in the literal sense of the story, but in terms of its larger theme and contemplations. Naslund believes, and so do I (our friendship started with these fascinations), that we are living in a revolutionary time, akin almost to the day when Copernicus proposed the notion that Earth circles the sun, and not the other way around.

Today, we're trying to comprehend the images from the Hubble telescope, overwhelming us since the early 1990s with photographs of faraway galaxies, and stars being born, and a comet colliding with the planet Jupiter. At first, we took it as a dazzling slide show, a kind of beauty we could not have imagined. Soon, however, another idea began to dawn, and as it slowly took an unwanted shape, we could feel a tearing at the edges of our minds. Hubble gave a face to the glory of the heavens, gave us a kaleidoscope of images suggesting what we had secretly feared, that we are, in fact, a flyspeck in the vastness. For suddenly we were seeing back into time, seeing galaxies a billion light-years away, which meant that the images themselves were a billion years old. And then the numbers began to seem real—real and impossible all at once, for in our galaxy the Sun is one of a hundred billion stars, and our Milky Way is a single galaxy among untold billions.

In the face of those overwhelming realities what do we believe? How do we comprehend our place in creation, and how should we feel if scientists close in—as they very well might in the next decade—on definitive proof of life in other places? Sena Naslund believes that for many of us those notions are so terrifying, so threatening to the Sunday school certainties on which we were raised, that we cling even harder to our old beliefs. She recalls the story of Galileo pointing his telescope at the Moon and seeing the craters that marred its face. Pope Urban VIII would have none of it. The idea that the Moon was flawed and not the perfect creation of God—combined with Galileo's endorsement of Copernicus—so horrified the Pope that he summoned the great Italian scientist to Rome and threatened him with torture if he didn't recant. Galileo recanted. But in the long run, of course, these events did nothing to diminish God; they simply made the Pope look foolish.

So it has always been with science, and so it is today, and Naslund wrote a novel about these things. On the surface, it is an adventure story set in the year 2020. An astrophysicist named Thom Bergmann, using new techniques of spectroscopic analysis, has found evidence of life in a distant galaxy—biomolecules, he believes, that could only be produced by living things. Such discoveries are plausible. Even today in the year 2012, scientists using the latest telescopes have found more than seven hundred exoplanets—planets orbiting other stars—and at least fifty of those are believed to be in the habitable zones, circling faraway suns at a distance that might allow for liquid water. Where there is water, there could be life, perhaps even in our own solar system. From Mars to Europa, the scientists are searching, while others are sifting through data from the new and powerful Kepler telescope, looking for planets that resemble our own.

For her novel, Naslund has picked the year 2020 as the moment of truth. Her character, Thom Bergmann, saves his data—his revolutionary proof of distant life—on a computer flash drive, which he entrusts temporarily to his wife. Lucy Bergmann wears the drive like a pendant around her neck, nestled lovingly between her breasts, and there it rests when her husband is killed. From this beginning, Naslund's story, which sounds fantastic in any kind of summary, assumes a plausibility of its own:

While fiercely guarding her husband's discoveries, Lucy is pursued by a group of extremists—an ecumenical collection of fundamentalists, Muslim, Jew, and Christian, who are willing to murder, if that's what it takes, in defense of the literal truth of religion. They are worried especially about the flash drive and the scientific knowledge it may contain, and about a simultaneous discovery, this one from the realm of archeology. In the perpetually war-torn Middle East, researchers have found an ancient text, something akin to the Dead Sea Scrolls, shedding new light on the Book of Genesis. This early author of the Genesis text, writing six hundred years before the birth of Christ, suggests that Creation should be understood, not through the analogy of the potter—God creating humans out of clay—but rather through a more familiar ritual, the timeless act of procreation.

> *In the beginning there was something*
> *and there was nothing.*
> *When they connected, there was everything.*
> *And it was everywhere.*

Did this writer from antiquity understand in his soul the scientific theory of the Big Bang—that when matter and anti-matter came together the universe was born? In her page-turning thriller about the bloody attempt to suppress such heresy, Naslund's story unfolds in places overflowing with symbolism: the Tigris and Euphrates rivers, the Olduvai Gorge where the early ancestors of humans evolved, the caves of France where the first human artists painted the walls.

> *. . . Shaggy bison and aurochs tossed their heads and stirred up dust with*
> *their trampling. Rounded horses shifted their haunches. Lions sped forward*
> *with faces like wedges among the herds, and elephantine mammoths moved*
> *with curtains of hair swaying from their sides.*
> *The contours of the cave, its bulges and declivities, helped to form their*
> *bodies, and the shifting shadows of those irregularities in the undulating light*
> *made the animals surge and retreat. Billows of calcite mimicked clouds . . .*
> *"Like constellations," Lucy said. "In the night sky, animals and giants*
> *populating the sky."*

Naslund's message in the course of these pages is that at least for the last thirty-five thousand years—the age of the paintings in the French cave—human beings have looked to the heavens to discover who they are, and this splendid yearning continues even now. It has often summoned the best that's within us—our poetry and art and theology and science—but it can also summon the worst, including our fears of the great unknown. As an artist herself, Naslund now offers the gift of mystery, an offering that almost certainly we will need in the face of discoveries in our own lifetime. She seems to be saying in this ambitious parable that when it comes to the inevitability of new truth—even when it flies in the face of the old—there is really no need to be afraid.

The Beat Goes On

FEATURING:

Admiral Robert Penn Warren and the Snows of Winter
—William Styron

Salvation on Sand Mountain—Dennis Covington

Brokeback Mountain—Annie Proulx

Unbroken—Laura Hillenbrand

ALSO, JOHN GRISHAM, KATHRYN STOCKETT, ISABEL
WILKERSON, DOT JACKSON, RON RASH, CHARLES FRAZIER,
ROBERT MORGAN, THOMAS MERTON, LEO TOLSTOY, LARRY
MCMURTRY, TOM PEACOCK, REBECCA SKLOOT

As I was nearing the end of writing this book, my friend Tom
Lawrence, a literary soul brother in Tennessee, called my attention
to *Admiral Robert Penn Warren and the Snows of Winter*, a tiny book
by William Styron. Published in 1978 by Palaemon Press in North
Carolina, it consists essentially of a single essay in which Styron proclaims his debt to Robert Penn Warren. Among other things in these

elegant pages, Styron remembers his discovery of *All the King's Men*, in 1947, during a blizzard in New York City.

Somehow the excitement of reading All the King's Men *is always linked in my mind with the howling blizzard outside and the snow piling up in a solid white impacted mass outside my basement window. The book itself was a revelation and gave me a shock to brain and spine like a freshet of icy water. I had of course read many novels before, including many of the greatest, but this powerful and complex story embedded in prose of such fire and masterful imagery—this, I thought with growing wonder, this was what a novel was all about, this was it, the bright book of life, what writing was supposed to be. When finally the blizzard stopped and the snow lay heaped on the city streets, silent as death, I finished* All the King's Men *as in a trance, knowing once and for all that I, too, however falteringly and incompletely, must try to work such magic. I began my first novel before that snow had melted; it is a book called* Lie Down in Darkness, *and in tone and style, as any fool can see, it is profoundly indebted to the work which so ravished my heart and mind during that long snowfall.*

Rarely, I think, has a writer captured more perfectly that rich and multilayered joy of discovery that comes to us periodically from books. As I read back over these accounts of my own discoveries, I can't help but notice that many of these books—though not all—were those I read when I was young. I suppose it's natural this would be the case. We are all more impressionable when we are young, more susceptible to new emotions and new ideas, but the beauty of it is the books keep coming. It's true that reading habits have changed; the clamor for simple entertainment or escape often seems more prevalent than the yearning for something that will touch the heart. And yet there are multiple examples to the contrary. John Grisham, a fine storyteller, has soared to the top of the best seller lists with books that put a human face on capital punishment and corporate irresponsibility. Kathryn Stockett's novel, *The Help*, became a number one *New York Times* best seller and Isabel Wilkerson's *The Warmth of Other Suns* won the National Book Critics' Circle Award for General Nonfiction, as they continue to explore the dilemmas of race.

And there are also surprises, the books that seem to come out of nowhere—books such as Dennis Covington's *Salvation on Sand Mountain*, a brilliant work of literary journalism which appeared in 1994. It was, looking back, part of a flood of Appalachian writing that has enriched the literary world for twenty years. Debut novels such as Dot Jackson's *Refuge* and Ron Rash's *One Foot in Eden* have won the sparkling acclaim they deserve, ranking with Charles Frazier's *Cold Mountain* or Robert Morgan's *Gap Creek* and *Boone*. But for me at least, none of these works has been more original, or more unexpected, than *Salvation on Sand Mountain*.

It's a book that I very well might have skipped if I had not been asked to review it. How much would I want to read, after all, about snake-handling cults in the lower Appalachians? But Covington told a gripping tale. It began, for him, with a newspaper assignment. The *New York Times* wanted a story about Glenn Summerford, a snake-handling preacher in northern Alabama who, in a drunken, jealous rage, forced his wife, Darlene, to thrust her hand into a cage of rattle-snakes. Summerford assumed that Darlene would die. Unfortunately for him she managed to survive the multiple bites, and Covington was dispatched to cover the trial. It was a lurid, sensational event in the hill-country town of Scottsboro, Alabama, an odd, discordant echo, perhaps, of a trial the town would prefer to forget (and a trial that as we saw in Chapter 2 influenced a young Harper Lee). In 1931, nine African American hoboes, soon to be known as the Scottsboro Boys, were arrested and falsely accused of rape, and their rapid convictions by an all-white jury left a permanent scar on the town's reputation. There was no such problem with the Summerford trial. The preacher was convicted of attempted murder, and the world at large was briefly intrigued, as it might have been by reports of a natural disaster or a massive train wreck. Covington, however, was transfixed, fascinated by this curious cult, which, at the very least, was not attractive to those of lesser faith.

In the beginning, he was appropriately skeptical of his subjects, offering this account of his initial encounter with Brother Charles McGlocklin, a man who would later become his friend.

"And I'll tell you something else," he said. "One night I was fasting and praying on the mountain, and I was taken out in the spirit. The Lord appeared to me in layers of light." His grip tightened on my shoulder. "He spoke a twelve-hour message to me on one word: polluted.*"*

"Polluted?"

"Yes. Polluted. Now, you think about that for a minute. A twelve-hour message."

I thought about it for a minute, and then decided Brother Charles was out of his mind.

But as the weeks and months went by and Covington set out on the snake-handling circuit, visiting churches in the mountains of northern Alabama, and in Georgia, Tennessee, Kentucky, and West Virginia, he found something contagious in the ardor of that worship; found himself wondering if what appeared at first to be nothing but hysteria, might conceivably be what the snake-handlers said it was: the Holy Spirit set loose in their midst. The Bible itself was certainly explicit.

And these signs shall follow them that believe; In my name shall they cast out devils; they shall speak with new tongues; They shall take up serpents; and if they drink any deadly thing, it shall not hurt them; they shall lay hands on the sick, and they shall recover.

Clearly, these people deep in the hills—worshipping, perhaps, in a converted gas station with a makeshift cross—believed the scriptures meant what they said. And there was something else as well. They seemed to Covington to be on a journey, some passionate rite of purification in a world so filled with unholy things. He soon discovered, after a dive into the genealogy of his family, that his own ancestors may have worshipped in churches such as these, and there came a time in the course of the book when he described the most unlikely of scenes.

Carl's eyes were saying, you. And yes, it was the big rattler, the one with my name on it, acrid-smelling, carnal, alive. And the look in Carl's eyes seemed to change as he approached me. He was embarrassed. The snake was all he had, his eyes seemed to say. But as low as it was, as repulsive, if I took it, I'd be possessing the sacred. Nothing was required except obedience. Nothing had to be given up except my own will. This was the moment. I didn't stop to think about it. I just gave in. I stepped forward and took the snake with both hands.

As I read Dennis Covington's remarkable tale I found myself thinking, improbably enough, about other books I had read on the subject of religion: the writings of Thomas Merton, perhaps, or Leo Tolstoy's *The Kingdom of God Is Within You*; books affirming that the journey of faith is not meant to be easy. But more concretely, I was simply in awe of Covington's achievement, this exercise in literary journalism, at once so personal and so ambitious. I have tried on occasion to do the same kind of work. I understand the difficulties of the form, and this, I thought, was journalism at its finest, a discovery of meaning, melodrama and heart in such an utterly unexpected place.

In recent years, only one other book has had this effect, has taken me so completely by surprise. It's one, in fact, that in the beginning was not a book at all, but rather a short story in the *New Yorker*. Published first in 1997, Annie Proulx's *Brokeback Mountain* flew under the radar for a few years, until Larry McMurtry, a writer of great western epics such as *Lonesome Dove*, turned it into a screenplay. After seeing the movie and being stunned especially by Heath Ledger's performance, surely one of the finest in the history of film, I wanted to see what Proulx had written. Her story by then had become a brief book, fifty-five pages about a pair of cowboys in the Rocky Mountain West. As the story begins, Ennis del Mar and Jack Twist are both in their teens, hired hands on a Wyoming sheep ranch. Sometime near the end of that first lonesome summer, just the two of them above the tree line, Jack and Ennis made love in their tent. It was not something either of them had planned.

"I'm not no queer," said Ennis.

"Me neither," said Jack.

They left the high country at the end of that summer, and both got married and began raising families. Four years passed but as soon as they saw each other again, they understood it was not a one-time thing—not some isolated moment on Brokeback Mountain. Theirs, they knew, was a bond to be ended only by death.

As the story unfolded in Annie Proulx's graceful prose, I was impressed anew by her remarkable act of literary courage. This was, after all, 2005, a time when homophobia was steeply on the rise. President George W. Bush had used it in his run for reelection, and a noisy minority of American Christians were railing against a sin their savior never mentioned. But Proulx's novella was more than a story of homosexuality. She was writing more broadly about longing and loss, an emptiness most of us try to keep at bay.

> *. . . he is suffused with a sense of pleasure because Jack Twist was in his dream. The stale coffee is boiling up but he catches it before it goes over the side, pours it into a stained cup and blows on the black liquid, lets a panel of the dream slide forward. If he does not force his attention on it, it might stoke the day, rewarm that old, cold time on the mountain when they owned the world and nothing seemed wrong. The wind strikes the trailer like a load of dirt coming off a dump truck, eases, dies, leaves a temporary silence.*

Writers have to write about these things, this dark underside of the human heart, for how else could it ever be transformed? But sometimes they write about other things, too, searching for redemption, even bits of heroism here or there. And so it was in 2011 that my friend Tom Peacock introduced me to yet another book. Peacock is one of my literary heroes, an author still writing beautifully at the age of ninety-two—a gift that is rooted in part, I think, in his voracious appetite as a reader. He told me he had just finished reading *Unbroken*, the latest best seller by Laura Hillenbrand, author of *Seabiscuit*. I had read *Seabiscuit*, liking it less than I thought I would, perhaps because of soaring expectations. (I may well have been a minority of one.) But for me *Unbroken* was a whole different matter; Peacock called it "perfectly marvelous," and I thought he was understating the case.

Hillenbrand spent seven years on the project, poring through old diaries and letters and conducting seventy-five interviews with her unlikely subject, Louie Zamperini, an Olympic track star turned war hero. She begins his story with a scene from the Pacific in World War II:

. . . Louie Zamperini lay across a small raft, drifting westward. Slumped alongside him was a sergeant, one of his plane's gunners. On a separate raft, tethered to the first, lay another crewman, a gash zigzagging across his forehead. Their bodies, burned by the sun and stained yellow from the raft dye, had withered down to skeletons. Sharks glided in lazy loops around them, dragging their backs along the rafts, waiting.

This is a book that captures the terrors of war, graphic, unsentimental, sketching the fury of America's enemy, the Japanese, an army motivated at least in part by the assumptions of racial superiority that Hitler was preaching half a world away. Through Hillenbrand, we feel the camaraderie of the American forces, the bravery of men like Louie Zamperini, and the impossible suffering they endured. More powerfully even than Tom Brokaw, Hillenbrand, with her meticulous research and storyteller's eye, shines new light on the greatness of the Greatest Generation.

A critic for *New York* magazine complained in mock frustration that *Unbroken* "seems designed to wrench from self-respecting critics all the blurby adjectives we normally try to avoid: It is amazing, unforgettable, gripping, harrowing, chilling, and inspiring." And Rebecca Skloot, herself a superb popular historian, called Hillenbrand simply "one of our best writers."

And so it is clear that for those of us who love a good book, the end of great writing is not in sight. We may, of course, have our different definitions of greatness, and those that I have confessed in these pages are deeply personal and purely my own. Not everyone is drawn to a book about war, not everyone will share my love of Southern writers or American journalists such as David Halberstam. And where are the authors from other lands? Where are Homer, Chaucer, Hemingway, or Proust? These are questions for which I have no answer. Only this: whatever the books that have touched our hearts—whether through joy, discomfort, inspiration or escape—those are the encounters that are worth celebrating, and preferences none of us need to defend.

Notes and Acknowledgments

E VEN THOUGH THESE pages are highly personal, reflecting my ruminations on the books that have mattered most in my life, I must also acknowledge a debt to other writers and friends who have helped to make this book what it is. In every chapter, there are quotes from the featured books—quotes acknowledged in the narrative itself, which are designed to convey the power and the beauty of these works. For the most part these quotes are self-explanatory.

In addition, in putting together the back-stories and reflecting critically on these books, I've relied on the insights of other authors. Here, chapter by chapter, are grateful acknowledgements of those debts.

Chapter 1—Two authors in particular helped shape my understanding of the writing of *Huckleberry Finn*. Robert G. O'Meally, Zora Neale Hurston Professor of Literature at Columbia University, provided an essay entitled "Blues for Huckleberry" as introduction to a 2003 Barnes & Noble Classics edition of *Adventures of Huckleberry Finn*. It was O'Meally who called my attention to the reflections of Toni Morrison and Ralph Ellison on the characters of Huck and Jim. O'Meally also quotes the oft-cited observation by Ernest Hemingway that "all American writing" comes from *Huckleberry Finn*. For a broader view of Mark Twain's life and the accumulation of experiences that shaped the writing of Twain's masterpiece, I relied on Ron Powers's biography, *Mark Twain: A Life*. And finally, I relied on the Roy Blount Jr. essay, "Mark Twain: Our Original Superstar," published in the July 3, 2008, issue of *Time*.

Chapter 2—For the background story of *To Kill a Mockingbird*, I am indebted to Charles J. Shields's biography of Harper Lee, *Mockingbird*. The stories of Tom Robertson and Walter Lett, two real-life victims of racial injustice who bear a resemblance to the fictional Tom Robinson, are both contained in *Mockingbird*. For the story of the Scottsboro Boys, perhaps the most famous example of injustice in the 1930s, I relied on Dan T. Carter's book, *Scottsboro: A Tragedy of the American South*; Douglas O. Linder's essay, "The Trials of 'The Scottsboro Boys'"; and the PBS documentary, *Scottsboro: An American Tragedy*, directed by Daniel Anker and Barak Goodman.

Richard Wright's review of *The Heart Is a Lonely Hunter* appeared in the *New Republic* in August 1940. The story of Lillian Smith's role in the arrest of Dr. Martin Luther King Jr., which indirectly influenced the presidential election of 1960, is told in Taylor Branch's *Parting the Waters: America in the King Years 1954–63*.

Chapter 3—Henry Louis Gates's phrase "incandescent with racial rage" appears in the book, *Albert Murray and the Aesthetic Imagination of a Nation*, edited by Barbara A. Baker. Gates's appraisals of Murray appear in that same volume. Biographical information on Richard Wright is based primarily on Wright's *Black Boy*. Historian Joel Williamson's quote about lynching comes from his book, *A Rage for Order*.

The story of James Baldwin's early life comes from Baldwin's *Notes of a Native Son*. In my 2008 book, *With Music and Justice for All*, I tell the story of Baldwin's encounter with school desegregation in Charlotte, North Carolina. Baldwin tells that story himself in "The Hard Kind of Courage," *Harper's Magazine*, October 1958. Albert Murray's quote,

"Boy, don't come telling me nothing about no old white folks," comes from Murray's "Stonewall Jackson's Waterloo," published in *Harper's*, February 1969. So does his quote about "grown folks talking."

Chapter 4—Larry L. King's profile of comedian Dave Gardner, "Whatever Happened to Brother Dave?," appeared in *Harper's* in September 1970. Part of King's story about his writing of "The Old Man" was related to me during a chance encounter with him in Washington, D.C., early in the 1970s. More formally, King told the story in *The Old Man and Lesser Mortals*. King's assessments of Willie Morris and David Halberstam are contained in his book, *In Search of Willie Morris*. Morris's account of his first meeting with Senator Robert Kennedy is contained in the memoir, *New York Days*. Tom Wolfe's description of Jimmy Breslin comes from Wolfe's *The New Journalism*. Robert Kennedy's remarkable speech after the death of Dr. Martin Luther King Jr., delivered extemporaneously, is quoted in the book, *RFK: Collected Speeches*, edited by Edwin O. Guthman and C. Richard Allen.

Chapter 5—Jacobo Timerman's description of the Ukranian village in which he was born is contained in his book, *Prisoner Without a Name, Cell Without a Number*. His powerful quotes about President Jimmy Carter and the "violent and criminal" twentieth century were offered in a 1985 interview with me and appear in my book, *Prophet from Plains: Jimmy Carter and His Legacy*. The story of Anne Frank and her family is taken substantially, of course, from *Anne Frank: The Diary of a Young Girl*. But I also relied on *Anne Frank Remembered: The Story of the Woman Who Helped Hide the Frank Family*, by Miep Gies and Alison Leslie Gold. Eleanor Roosevelt's quote about Anne Frank comes from Roosevelt's introduction to the 1993 Bantam Books edition of Frank's diary. Kurt Vonnegut's wartime letter written to his family on May 29, 1945, appears in his *Armageddon in Retrospect*. So does his original description of the bombing of Dresden. Marshall Frady's quote from an Egyptian editor about the dangers of America's role in the world appears in Frady's *Billy Graham: A Parable of American Righteousness*.

Chapter 6—President Woodrow Wilson's description of *The Birth of a Nation*—"like writing history with lightning"—appears in Joel Williamson's *A Rage for Order*. The story of Martin Luther King Sr.'s appearance at the 1976 Democratic National Convention comes from my own *Prophet from Plains*. On a couple of occasions, I've had the pleasure of interviewing Clyde Edgerton at some length about his writing, and those interviews, in addition to his novel *Walking Across Egypt*, form the backdrop of the Edgerton section in this chapter. In the course of many conversations, my friend Dori Sanders has recounted the writing of her blockbuster, *Clover*.

Chapter 7—Paul Kingsbury's "Pride and Prejudice," which appeared in the Fall 2003 issue of *Vanderbilt Magazine*, offers excellent insight into the Fugitive poets and the agrarians who wrote *I'll Take My Stand*. My synopsis here of the story of Huey Long is based primarily on three sources: T. Harry Williams's biography, *Huey Long*; Alan Brinkley's *Voices of Protest: Huey Long, Father Coughlin and the Great Depression*; and Ken Burns's PBS documentary, *Huey Long*. The quote about Long from President Roosevelt's mother, "Who is that awful man?," is taken from Brinkley's *Voices of Protest*. Arthur Schlesinger's disparaging quote about Long comes from an on-camera interview in Burns's documentary.

Chapter 8—Merle Haggard's lyrics about migrant workers in California are from the song, "Hungry Eyes." John Steinbeck's journalistic essays have been reprinted in the book, *The Harvest Gypsies: On the Road to the Grapes of Wrath*, with an insightful introduction by Charles Wollenberg. Dorothea Lange's quotes about her iconic photograph, "The Migrant Mother," are taken from her field notes. I benefited enormously from Robert DeMott's introduction to the Penguin edition of *The Grapes of Wrath*. DeMott, in turn, relied on Steinbeck's diary, *Working Days*, where Steinbeck's quotes and doubts about his novel were recorded. Critics' quotes about *The Grapes of Wrath*—both positive and negative—come from DeMott's introduction. Wayne Flynt's observations about *The Grapes of Wrath* were offered in an email exchange with me. Flynt's quotes about the treatment of poor whites in American literature comes from his excellent history, *Poor But Proud*. Bruce Springsteen's lyrics are taken from the song, "The Ghost of Tom Joad."

Dee Brown's *Bury My Heart at Wounded Knee* has helped to inspire a whole generation of books sympathetic to the story of American Indians. Two of my favorites are John Ehle's novelized history of the Cherokees, *Trail of Tears*, and Josephine Humphreys's haunting novel, *Nowhere Else on Earth*.

Chapter 9—Alex Haley tells the backstory of *Roots* in the final chapters of that book. C. Eric Lincoln's story of being attacked as a teenager appears in my book, *With Music and Justice for All*, and originally appeared in a 1988 profile of Lincoln that I wrote for the *Charlotte Observer*. The same profile included Alex Haley's assessment of Lincoln's fine novel, *The Avenue, Clayton City*. Rick Bragg's assessment of *Roots* was taken from an interview with me. Pat Conroy's beautiful essay, "The Death of Santini," was reprinted in the book, *Novello: Ten Years of Great American Writing*, published in 2000 by Novello Festival Press.

Chapter 10—Sena Jeter Naslund shared the stories behind her novels in a lengthy 2012 interview with me. An excellent profile of Naslund also appears in Roy Hoffman's *Alabama Afternoons: Profiles and Conversations*. John Updike's observations on Hester Prynne, protagonist of *The Scarlet Letter*, are taken from the National Public Radio essay, "Hester Prynne: Sinner, Victim, Object, Winner," by

Andrea Seabrook. Accounts of the Birmingham church bombing and the discovery of the patent leather shoe appear in Diane McWhorter's *Carry Me Home* and in my own *Cradle of Freedom: Alabama and the Movement That Changed America*. Geraldine Brooks's quotes about her protagonist Anna Frith, and about the human heart, are taken from an interview with Brooks included in the Penguin edition of *Year of Wonders*. Maureen Morehead's poem, cited by Sena Jeter Naslund, appears in the book, *In a Yellow Room*. Morehead is poet laureate of Kentucky.

Epilogue—In this epilogue of writers who continue to inspire me, I wanted to work in my fellow Alabamians, Tom Franklin, Michael Knight, Vicki Covington, Nanci Kincaid, Roy Hoffman, Cassandra King, and Mark Childress; South Carolinians Ashley Warlick and George Singleton; and North Carolinians Jerry Bledsoe and Hal Crowther. They are now, as they should be, officially included.

And finally for reading all or parts of this manuscript and offering valuable feedback, special thanks to my wife, Nancy Gaillard, and friends Jay Lamar, Tom Lawrence, Patti Meredith, Kathryn Scheldt, and Tom Peacock. Thanks also to Jacquelyn Hall, Steve Trout, Ellen Holliday, Tom Pinckney, Jennifer Lindsay, Becky McLaughlin, Mara Kozelsky, and Carol Sherrod.

Literary Index

C

D